this could scarcely escape being an object of curiosity. Fr. the neighbors I learned that he thought himself the richest & most learned man in the world—that he had been all his life time buying the small stones that are found in clams & oysters wh. he believed to be pearls—making to lose out of lead, & gold out of stone—that his father once possessed a small property but had lost it by indulging Eddard in his chimerical pursuits. All this only stimulated my desire of further acquaintance & it was not long ere I paid Eddard a visit. As I entered his residence—it was a miserable old hovel on a marsh at the head of a small cove wh. was washed away in a freshet a few years since, I beheld an old man who had nearly attained his ninetieth year, seated astraddle on a bench & cutting poles wh. a drawing knife. This was the father of Eddard & they both obtained their subsistence chiefly by the f old man's labours tho' in small part also by Eddard's hawking about the country a quantity of dry leaves wh. he very carefully cured every year wh. he believed himself & convinced some others to be the real tea plant. & This he preferred himself to the choicest Imperial but as the old women in the neighborhood were obstinate in their preference for the cheapest Bohea his sales were not very extensive. I accosted the old man & asked if Eddard were in: "Who's that wants me? was uttered in a squeaky voice from the only adjoining apartment. I turned my steps

Page from Seabury's *Autobiographical Sketch*, found in the Seabury Family Papers and deposited in The New-York Historical Society

Moneygripe's Apprentice

The Personal Narrative of Samuel Seabury III

Edited by Robert Bruce Mullin

Yale University Press • New Haven and London

The illustrations on pages 1 and 41 are taken from Edward Hazen, *The Panorama of Professions and Trades,* first published in 1836 and reprinted in 1970 by Century House, Watkins Glenn, New York. Reproduced by courtesy of Century House, Publishers.

Designed by Jo Aerne and set in Bembo type by Keystone Typesetting, Inc., Orwigsburg, Pennsylvania. Printed in the United States of America by BookCrafters, Inc., Chelsea, Michigan.

Library of Congress Cataloging-in-Publication Data
Seabury, Samuel.
Moneygripe's apprentice : the personal narrative of Samuel Seabury III / edited by Robert Bruce Mullin.
p. cm.
Includes index.
ISBN 0–300–04379–1
1. Seabury, Samuel. 2. New York (N.Y.)—Biography. 3. Apprentices—New York (N.Y.) 4. Editors—New York (N.Y.) 5. United States—Intellectual life—1783–1865. I. Mullin, Robert Bruce. II. Title.
F128.44.S4 1989   88–26182
974.7′103′0924—dc19   CIP

The paper in this book meets the guidelines for permanence and durability of the Committee on Production Guidelines for Book Longevity of the Council on Library Resources.

10 9 8 7 6 5 4 3 2 1

Contents

Acknowledgments

Only through the encouragement and assistance of many individuals and institutions is this long-forgotten manuscript now seeing the light of day. I wish to thank the owner of the original, the New-York Historical Society, and Mr. John Seabury for their permission to publish this edition. A further thanks must also be extended to the Society's archivist, Thomas E. Dunning, for his unfailing helpfulness. The staffs of the New York Public Library, New-York Historical Society Library, Duke University libraries, D. H. Hill Library of North Carolina State University, and Yale University libraries have all gone to great lengths in helping to solve some of the puzzles posed by Seabury's text. Furthermore, the staff members of the Yale Divinity Library have been gracious hosts during two summer research stints there.

I am deeply appreciative of the help of many persons in the field. Two of my colleagues here at North Carolina State, William Adler and Tony Stewart, both read and cogently criticized this work, while a third, Deborah Wyrick, helped clarify some obscure references. William Adler has furthermore helped me in translating some of Seabury's Latin passages. Others, such as George Lindbeck, George Marsden, David Myers, James VanderKam, and William Silva have all contributed, through their generous conversations, in sharpening my thought. Finally, I wish to thank Harry Stout of Yale University for his enthusiastic support of the work.

I am indebted to North Carolina State University for a faculty research grant that allowed me two summers of uninterrupted labor. I am further indebted to the Department of Philosophy and Religion here for providing such a congenial environment for research.

Viola Mullin has (as always) shown encouragement and support,

Acknowledgments

and has never flagged in her belief that Seabury's story was worth telling. Finally, Elizabeth Anne Mullin has taught me in sundry ways about the subtleties of the parent-child relationship and shown me that parenting, like everything else in this world, has two handles.

PART ONE

Editor's Introduction

"To be burnt" instructed the author on the last page of his manuscript, an account of his early years. Why, one cannot be certain. It may have opened too many old wounds or stirred too many long-settled memories for the successful religious journalist, theologian, and ecclesiastical leader. Perhaps, its tone echoed too distinctly of pain, doubt, and frustration. Perhaps the sixty-three-year-old author simply thought it best not to remember the anxieties of so long ago. The manuscript was not burned, however, and although short (106 pages) and covering only six years, the memoirs of Samuel Seabury offer a lucid insight into the social and religious world of the second decade of the nineteenth century as well as telling the moving account of one young man's coming of age.

When Samuel Seabury is remembered (and when he is not confused with his more famous grandfather also named Samuel Seabury) he is usually described as a bright, active clergyman of middling rank from a notable family. Historians regularly include him in any discussion of the influence of the Tractarian or Oxford Movement in America, and occasionally mention him as one of the last northern ecclesiastical defenders of the institution of slavery. But on the whole his life has held little attraction for scholars. Few besides those interested in the history of nineteenth-century Episcopalianism have concerned themselves with his life, and even for these few Seabury remains an eminently proper if perhaps stuffy cleric. Thus the surprise when one opens his unpublished and long-forgotten autobiographical sketch and discovers a passionate account of his attempt between 1814 and 1821 to find a place for himself in the new American society. Artfully combining pathos and humor, he chronicles his various adventures and mishaps and describes a world of workshops and apprentices, school teachers and countryfolk.

Standard references generally depict Seabury's life as not unlike

that of other clergymen of the period.[1] He was born in New London, Connecticut, in 1801 into a clerical family that boasted of including the first bishop of the Episcopal Church in America. Largely
self-educated, he received an M.A. degree from Columbia University, *honoris causa,* in 1823. Before following his family tradition and
entering the ministry, he gained a fine local reputation as a teacher at
a school loosely associated with St. Ann's Episcopal Church in
Brooklyn.[2] After his ordination to the priesthood in 1828 he served
in a number of small churches before becoming an instructor at the
innovative Flushing Institute in Flushing, New York, founded by
William Augustus Muhlenberg. At the Flushing Institute, Seabury
and the other instructors attempted to instill in their students a firm
foundation in the classics while still providing an education flexible
enough for either the counting house or college.[3] Seabury himself
defended the usefulness of classical education in one of his earliest
published works, *The Study of the Classics on Christian Principles*
(1831). In 1833 he began his long tenure as editor of the New-York-
based *Churchman,* and he became—through his insightful and at
times acerbic comments on the religious happenings of the period—
one of the major ecclesiastical journalists of the first half of the
nineteenth century. In this role he defended the peculiar doctrines

1. The only biographical sketches we have of Seabury are the following: Samuel
Roosesvelt Johnson, *A Discourse . . . at the Church of the Annunication, City of New
York, on the 25th day of June, A.D., 1873, in Memory of Samuel Seabury, D.D., Presbyter
of the Diocese of New York, Professor of Biblical Learning and Interpretation of Scripture in
the General Theological Seminary* ([New York], [1873]); William J. Seabury, "Members of the Seabury Family," *American Church Review* 46 (1885): 62–74; Arthur
Adams, "The Seabury Family," *Historical Magazine of the Protestant Episcopal Church* 3
(1934): 123–32; and the article by Edward R. Hardy, Jr., in the *Dictionary of American
Biography.* For a discussion of his public career, see Robert Bruce Mullin, *Episcopal
Vision/American Reality: High Church Theology and Social Thought in Evangelical America* (New Haven, Conn.: Yale University Press, 1986).

2. For Seabury's reputation as an educator, see Ralph Foster Ward, *Brooklyn
Village: 1816–1834* (New York: Columbia University Press, 1938), 182.

3. On the Flushing Institute, see Alvin W. Skardon, *Church Leader in the Cities:
William Augustus Muhlenberg* (Philadelphia: University of Pennsylvania Press, [1971]),
60–71.

and practices of the Episcopal Church (such as apostolic succession and the use of a set liturgy) and attacked the excesses of evangelical Protestantism. Later, as an early proponent of the Oxford movement's attempt to reawaken Catholic principles within Anglicanism, he defended the rightness of true Catholicism against the corrupted Church of Rome.

During his editorship he also set forth his central contribution to the theological debate of the time in a subtle essay entitled "Salvability of the Heathen," a subject upon which he elaborated in successive articles. In contrast to both Calvinists (who believed that those who never heard the Christian message would be damned) and Universalists (who believed in universal salvation), Seabury argued that the salvation of "heathen"[4] individuals was *possible* (but not inevitable) by means of the universal power of Christ's atonement. This salvation was conditioned, however, upon their sincere obedience to the law that God had implanted in their nature, which Seabury described as "the God of their hearts, manifesting himself by a light of the mind, by instincts of goodness, by a sensibility of quilt, by awakenings and warnings of conscience."[5] American Protestants erred, he continued, in viewing justification as an instantaneous occurrence rather than as a gradual process brought about by the free human will's continuing response to divine grace. Seabury is also usually remembered for his long (1838–68) and distinguished service as rector of the Church of the Annunication in New York City where he attempted to put into practice many of these ideas of Catholic practice and Christian nurture.

Finally, most biographical notes on Seabury record that he was professor of biblical learning at the General Theological Seminary in New York from 1862 until his death. In all the published accounts of his life Seabury appears as a conscientious and diligent cleric with

---

4. American Protestant writers at the time termed as heathen all those who had never heard the Christian gospel.

5. "The Nature and the Extent of the Redemption of Mankind by Jesus Christ Stated and Explained." *Churchman* 8 (Sept. 8, 1838): 101.

keen interests in education, the question of universal salvation, and the importance of volition in religious growth. Other than that his life is seen as ordinary, and, considering his familial line, horribly predictable. None of his biographers, save one, make mention of his early years, before his decision to enter into the ministerial profession of his father and grandfather. His eulogist made one passing allusion: that for a time Seabury made "an unsuccessful essay in our Great Master's guild."[6]

His unpublished manuscript, however, is principally an account of this "unsuccessful essay." Written in 1831, the work recounts Seabury's early years, and from the story told in its pages his life is shown to have been anything but staid and ordinary. Born into genteel poverty as a result of both the Revolutionary War and the weaknesses in the character of his clerical father, Seabury was unable to secure the classical education that might have ensured his social advancement. Instead he found himself apprenticed to a furniture maker. Yet he felt at home neither in the workshop where he labored nor in the elegant drawing rooms of the wealthy relatives whom he visited. In his narrative he describes himself as a young man constitutionally unable to fit into either the social order of the day, his notable familial heritage, or even into the religious universe inherited from his family. His story is accordingly an account of his attempt to find a place for himself. On the most basic level, this entailed securing a livelihood that might support him and allow for his advance, but it also concerned his working out a new understanding of the nature of society and of the universe.

The larger issue of the narrative, however, is the reconciliation of freedom and providence on the social, psychological, and cosmic levels. His quest drove him at one point toward Roman Catholicism and at another to philosophical materialism, while all the time leading him to ponder the fundamental nature of the universe. These are

6. Johnson, *Discourse*, 13–14.

the incidents he relates and the questions with which he grapples in his memoirs. They are interesting in part because they are the questions asked by every individual reaching maturity in order to reconcile himself with the world as it is. They are also of interest because they elucidate aspects of Seabury's later career. His devotion to the classics becomes understandable in light of their importance to him as an avenue of advance; his interest in things Catholic takes on new significance from the perspective of his early attraction to Rome; and his great concern for freedom, will, and grace can be seen as a lifelong working out of the religious questions of the workhouse. Finally, the experiences he relates are interesting because they elucidate an underlying cleavage between the religious spirit of the eighteenth century and that of the nineteenth.

Background

Seabury's narrative cannot be fully understood divorced from its context. It presupposes a knowledge of the Anglican religious world and the Seabury family's role in it. Furthermore, the narrative takes place within the vortex of social forces that were quickly making America of the early national period (1789–1832) a very different society than it had been.

Anglicans during the late colonial era had seen themselves, to one degree or another, as a branch of the Church of England in the new world that reflected psychologically as well as institutionally its English heritage. The Church of England during this period still understood itself as an integral part of the fabric of society and not merely as a narrow religious community. The church was governed by descending offices of authority: metropolitans (archbishops), bishops, priests, and deacons. And just as God had ordered the church hierarchically, so too had he ordered the state. The stratification of the social order was, therefore, neither an accident of history nor a working out of mindless economic forces, but rather a social system as God had planned it. The British constitution in particular reflected this organic, hierarchical order. A monarch governed through a parliament of lords and commons representing the various orders of the realm. The church took its place in this parliment. Its bishops were lords spiritual and shared the upper house with the lords temporal, and together they guided the course of the realm.

Since the social order was seen as shaped by God, to deny or, worse, to overturn that order was not only rebellion but also an action bordering on blasphemy. To be sure, it was well recognized that this vision fell apart in a reality where faction played its role in both church and society, real power operated along far less idealistic avenues, and church and realm (as in the case of the Nonjurors) could as easily come to blows as work in tandem. Nonetheless, throughout the eighteenth century this vision continued to have a mythic power that should not be underestimated. Many public rituals still reflected it; the official teachings of the Church of England reinforced it; and established formularies such as the catechism (found in every copy of the Anglican prayer book and memorized by all devout children) gave it its classic expression:

> My duty . . . [is] to honour and obey the King, and all that are put in authority under him: To submit myself to all my governours, teachers, spiritual pastors and masters: To order myself lowly and reverently to all my betters: To hurt nobody by word nor deed: To be true and just in all my dealing: To bear no malice nor hatred in my heart: To keep my hands from picking and stealing, and my tongue from evil-speaking, lying and slandering: To keep my body in temperance, soberness and chastity: Not to covet nor desire other men's goods; but to learn and labour truly to get mine own living, and to do my duty in that state of life, unto which it shall choose God to call me.

It is not surprising, then, that as the century ended, and as the British order found itself threatened by the ideological rumblings from rev-

olutionary France, the church saw itself as a bulwark of the established order and an opponent of the new republican spirit.[7]

Colonial Anglicans on the whole shared in this vision. Rhys Issac
has shown how such a vision linked together church and state in
prerevolutionary Virginia.[8] In the northern colonies the political
reality of an overwhelmingly non-Anglican population dampened
the vision, but many Anglican clergy continued to hope that better
times lay in the future. Particularly after 1763, with the triumph of
the British cause over the French and along with it the increased
attempts to integrate the American colonies more closely into the
English system, many hoped for a more complete "anglicizing" of
American life. Northern church leaders such as Samuel Johnson,
first president of King's (later Columbia) College had repeatedly
argued that a vigorous church headed by bishops was a necessary
step in securing a closer relationship between colony and mother
country.

> [T]he most effectual method to secure our dependence on the
> Crown of Great Britian would be to render our constitution
> here, both in church and state, as near as possible comfortable
> to that our our mother-country, and consequently to send us
> wise and good bishops to be at the head of our ecclesiastical
> affairs, as well as governors (and I could wish a Viceroy) to

7. For recent discussions of this eighteenth-century Anglican social vision, see J.
P. Kenyon, *Revolution Principles: The Politics of Party, 1689–1720* (Cambridge: Cambridge University Press, 1977), 83–101; and Peter Nockles, "Pusey on the Question
of Church and State," in Perry Butler, ed., *Pusey Rediscovered* (London: SPCK, 1983),
255–97. On the Anglican response to the social and political disturbances of the era of
the French Revolution, see, for example, the discussion in R. A. Soloway, *Prelates and
People: Ecclesssiastical Social Thought in England, 1783–1852* (Toronto: University of
Toronto Press, 1969), 19–45; William R. Ward, *Religion and Society in England, 1790–
1850* (London: B. T. Batsford, 1972), 21–53; and Ford K. Brown, *Fathers of the
Victorians: The Age of Wilberforce* (Cambridge: Cambridge University Press, 1961),
passim.

8. Rhys Isaac, *The Transformation of Virginia, 1740–1790* (Chapel Hill: University
of North Carolina Press, 1982), 58–65.

represent his most sacred Majesty in the affairs of civil government.[9]

The debates of the 1760s over stamps and bishops led to the Revolutionary War of the 1770s and with the Treaty of Paris (1783) it became clear that the dreams of men like Samuel Johnson had been irreparably shattered. The few colonial Anglican establishments were quickly terminated, and little if any hope remained for a restoration of the old order. Many of those who had shared the older vision fled to Britian, Canada, or other parts of the empire. But those who stayed faced the task of picking up the pieces. Between 1784 and 1789, the remains of the colonial churches were reformed into the Protestant Episcopal Church in the United States of America. In its structure the American church was distinctly different from its English root. Its government was in large part a result of the triumphant republican spirit of the revolutionary period. Laity were given equal status with clergy in one house of its General Convention, and an absolute veto power was awarded over the newly created bishops. Perhaps the most profound change, though, was reflected in the name itself. The Church *of* England had become the Protestant Episcopal Church *in* the United States of America. The notion of a church that included the entire realm was replaced by the recognition that this new church was simply one among many. Both social status and psychological self-understanding were to be different in the new republic.

Few examples better illustrate how these political events could affect individual lives than does the history of the Seabury family.[10]

9. Samuel Johnson to John Potter, May 3, 1737 in *Samuel Johnson . . . His Career and Writings,* ed. Herbert and Carol Schneider, 4 vols. (New York: Columbia University Press, 1929), 1:88.

10. Details on the Seabury family history can be found in Arthur Adams, "The Seabury Family"; E. E. Beardsley, *Life and Correspondence of the Right Reverend Samuel Seabury D.D.* (Boston: Houghton, Mifflin and Co., 1881); and Bruce Steiner, *Samuel Seabury, 1729–1796: A Study in the High Church Tradition* (Athens: Ohio University Press, 1971). A manuscript history of the Seabury family, compiled by William J. Seabury (son of Samuel [III]) is in the possession of the New-York Historical Society.

Seaburys had long been part of the landscape of Puritan New England. In 1639 a John "Seaberry" purchased a house and garden in Boston, and, with the exception of John Seaberry's short residence in Barbados, the Seaburys continued to live and work in Massachusetts and Connecticut for generations. Most were like the substantial farmer and cooper Deacon John Seabury (c. 1673–1759) in their combination of solid piety with a loyalty to the church of the New England fathers. Even in the choice of a wife—Elizabeth Alden, a descendant of John Alden—Deacon John Seabury seemed firmly embedded in the world of New England Puritanism.

The course of the family, however, took a decided turn during the lifetime of Deacon John's fourth son, the first to be named Samuel (1706–64). The first of the Seabury line to attend college, Samuel enrolled at Yale College and was at the commencement of 1722 when the rector of the college, Timothy Cutler, a former tutor, Samuel Johnson, and the other "Yale Apostates" announced their decision to abandon Congregationalism and to seek episcopal orders in the Church of England. Deacon John, convinced that Yale was not a safe environment for a young man (particularly not for a young man preparing for the Congregational ministry), removed his son from temptation and entered him instead at Harvard College, where he graduated with the class of 1724. Through 1729 Seabury did all those things which candidates for the ministry at that time were supposed to do after graduation. He became duly licensed and "candidated" or preached in various congregations while awaiting a permanent call and ordination. A call eventually did come to a congregation in North Yarmouth in what is now Maine. Yet, early in 1730, Seabury reached a decision that was to affect his family's fortune for generations; he abandoned the Congregational church of his heritage and applied to enter the ministry of the Church of England. After traveling to England he was ordained in August of that year and returned to New London, Connecticut, as a missionary for the Society for the Propagation of the Gospel (SPG).

Why Seabury made his decision is open to interpretation. In part, like the Yale Apostates, he may have been influenced by the historical claims of the episcopal apologists. For almost a century Anglican writers had scoured the records of the early church in order to show that episcopal polity was the original church order, and hence the only sure foundation for church government. In part his choice may have been reflective of a disillusionment with Congregationalism, prompted (according to one account) over difficulties in collecting his salary while candidating.[11] Finally the influence of his wife, Abigail Mumford, and her family—all strong Episcopalians—quite likely also played a role in his decision. Whatever the cause, the result was that he (and his family's fortune) became set on a different path from that of the majority of his neighbors.

Seabury served in New London and preached in other mission stations in Connecticut as an SPG missionary before becoming rector of a church in Hempstead, Long Island. It was in this clerical world, that his son, the second Samuel Seabury (1729–96), who had been born just before his father's momentous decision, was brought up. The younger Samuel also chose the ministry for his career, though he also studied medicine. He graduated from Yale College in 1748 and was ordained by the bishop of London in 1753. Continuing in his father's footsteps, he served as an SPG missionary in New Jersey, Long Island, and Westchester county, New York. His lot, however, was not to be that of a quiet person.

As a result of his involvement in the revolutionary events of the 1760s and 1770s Seabury found himself cast in an increasingly prominent role as one of his church's (and eventually one of his king's) chief defenders. In the 1760s he joined with other clergy in the campaign to secure an American bishopric, and he actively participated in the controversy the plan provoked. In the 1770s, as the relationship between the crown and the colonies continued to deteriorate, he sharply criticized the movement toward independence, and, writing

11. Clifford K. Shipton in his article on Samuel Seabury (I) in *Sibley's Harvard Graduates* . . . (Boston: Massachusetts Historical Society, 1873–), 7:433–34 argues for such a motive, but Steiner (in *Seabury,* 14) vigorously denies it.

under the pseudonym "A. W. Farmer," he published some of the most effective loyalist tracts. Early in the war he was imprisoned by patriot forces. Eventually, he was forced to flee from his home to the safety of the British lines. There he served as a missionary on Staten Island, while acting as a chaplain to both a British man of war and the King's American Regiment, a loyalist force. For his loyalty to the British cause he was awarded, among other things, an honorary doctorate of divinity from Oxford. All of these actions linked Seabury's star even more closely to the British cause. He probably could not have helped but think of the parallels between the events of the 1770s and those of the great English struggle of the 1640s that pitted church and king against puritan and parliament. Despite the bleakness of the Commonwealth period, church and crown ultimately triumphed. Every May 29, the restoration of Charles II continued to be a day of thanksgiving in the church when it was recalled,

O Lord of our salvation, who hast been exceedingly gracious unto this land, and by thy miraculous providence didst deliver us out of our miserable confusions; by restoring to us, and to his own just and undoubted Rights, our then most gracious Sovereign Lord, King *Charles* the Second, notwithstanding all the power and malice of his enemies; and, by placing him on the Throne of these Kingdoms didst restore also unto us the publick and free profession of thy true Religion and Worship, together with our former Peace and Prospserity, to the great comfort and joy of our hearts: We are here now before thee, with all due thankfulness, to acknowledge thine unspeakable goodness herein, as upon this day shewed unto us, and to offer unto thee our sacrifice of praise for the same; humbly beseeching thee to accept this our unfeigned, though unworthy oblation of ourselves; vowing all holy obedience in thought, word, and work, unto thy Divine Majesty; and promising all loyal and dutiful Allegiance to thine Anointed Servant now set over us, and to his heirs after him; whom we beseech thee to bless with all increase of grace, honour and happiness, in this world, and to crown him with immortality and glory in the world to come.

Indeed, Seabury even named one of his sons, born on that date, Charles, in honor of the event—and perhaps almost as a pledge of his confidence in the old order. With the Restoration those loyal to the cause were remembered, and if the British eventually triumphed in the American war, his majesty's loyal church in all probability would be similarly rewarded. The result of the war might be an American episcopate to be filled by those loyal to church and king. Even advancement to the level of lord spiritual was not beyond the realm of hope. Any or all of these thoughts may have occupied Seabury's mind as he dutifully prayed for the king and awaited the outcome of the war.

Yorktown and eventually the Treaty of Paris put an end to such hopes. There would be no Restoration. America was not to develop along English lines. Church and realm would no longer be spiritually united. A place for the church had to be found in the new order. Seabury, as is well known, played a central role in this reorganization. In 1783 he was elected bishop by the Episcopal clergy of Connecticut and proceeded to England to secure consecration. Refused by the bishops of England, who could not waive the oath of allegiance required in all such consecrations and who furthermore expressed concern about his support at home, Seabury secured consecration from Nonjuring Scottish bishops in 1784. He returned to America and worked diligently in organizing the Episcopal Church in Connecticut and Rhode Island, as well as leaving his mark in numerous ways upon the formation of the national church. Yet his leadership in a small and struggling church brought little of the affluence or social advance that it would have if the war had turned out otherwise.[12] What he left to his son Charles was an honored

12. On the financial position of Seabury see, Robert A. Hallam, *Annal of St. James' Church, New London, for One Hundred and Fifty Years* (Hartford, Conn., 1873), 80–81. Even while serving as a bishop Seabury was apparently looked down upon by another

name, but little more. Charles Seabury, who also served in the ministry, spent his career in small and relatively insignificant churches in Connecticut and Long Island.

All of this family background with the "what ifs" and "might have beens" is essential to an understanding of *Moneygripe's Apprentice*. Charles Seabury was the father of the third Samuel Seabury, the author of the narrative. As his name symbolically reflected, Charles Seabury was a man who never successfully adapted to the new order. He lived his life as the old catechism directed, doing his duty in that state of life to which it had pleased God to call him. God for some reason had placed the Seabury fortune in this reduced state, and hence one's Christian duty was to make the best of one's lot. This trust in providence was the philosophy by which Charles Seabury lived and reared his children, and it was this passive personal philosophy of life that the younger Seabury ultimately could not reconcile with his own sense of personal ambition.

The troubled relationship between Seabury and his father is one dominant theme underlying the narrative. Yet in rejecting his father's counsel Seabury was forced to search out a more suitable social vision, and this quest is another theme. The questions of human freedom, divine providence, and the nature of the human predicament reverberate throughout the text. Seabury was ruefully aware of how contingent the human situation was, and how an individual's lot was so often dependent on factors beyond one's control. In his own life, for example, he recognized that had the events of history turned out slightly differently he might have found himself born into a socially prominent family, and hence his entrance into society and his securing of a successful career would have been matters of course. The actual events proved cruelly otherwise, and Seabury found himself instead relegated to the workshop. As much as he resented his fate, however, it also raised for him a wider question: was there any

member of the episcopate, Samuel Provoost of New York, because of his humble social background. See, James Eliot Lindsley, *This Planted Vine: A Narrative History of the Episcopal Diocese of New York* (New York: Harper and Row, 1984), 70.

divine plan for the world? Both his father and grandfather had felt at home in the universe largely because they believed that the universe made sense. The world of young Seabury bore little if any resemblance to the structured social order presupposed by the religion of his forefathers. Thus, instead of simply inheriting the older vision, Seabury was forced to make his own sense of the rough and tumble world of the early nineteenth century.

From one perspective Seabury's challenge was far from unique. Numerous scholars have suggested that in the early national period the social implications of the Revolutionary settlement were worked out. Class divisions indeed continued to exist, and particularly in the cities genteel folk still referred to mechanics and tradesmen as "the inferior order of people."[13] At the same time, one great hallmark of these years was a sense of social confusion stemming from, as Gordon Wood has suggested, a crisis of authority. Broadly speaking, the old colonial order found itself superseded by a new one emphasizing economic individualism and social fluidity. Old institutions—such as apprenticeship, which in an earlier age had been as important as a means of social control as economic production—were left in a chaotic state. How to reestablish a social order for the new era was the concern of many in the first two decades of the century. By the 1830s a new order, resting upon revivalistic piety, Scottish Common Sense Philosophy, and the moral and educational accomplishments of the Second Great Awakening was largely in place. Yet, unlike earlier orders, it was based, at least in principle, on individual choice and decision, not social circumstance. What one was in the society was determined to a great degree by what one made of oneself, not whence one had come.[14]

13. Howard B. Rock, *Artisans of the Republic: The Tradesmen in New York City in the Age of Jefferson* (New York: New York University Press, 1979), 3. For a general background to the social milieu, see Rowland T. Berthoff, *An Unsettled People: Social Order and Disorder in American History* (New York: Harper and Row, 1971), and Jackson Turner Main, *The Social Structure of Revolutionary America* (Princeton: Princeton University Press, 1965).

14. Gordon Wood, *The Creation of the American Republic, 1776–1787* (New York: W.

Editor's Introduction

Few groups, then, bore the responsibility of making sense of this new world more heavily than the young who were coming of age. The open, early national society provided opportunity and freedom, but it also, conversely, complicated the passage into adulthood. Many factors, such as extended families and established communities, which had traditionally helped ease the way for a youth's entrance into adult society, were now no longer so available. The great population migration of the period, fueled by individuals continually seeking better places to make their fortunes, inevitably weakened the kin network, and where it remained the changed social circumstances lessened the power of familial precedent to serve as a sure guide for the rising generation. Indeed, the cultural emphasis on individual choice tended to thrust upon the shoulders of the young the primary responsibility of coming to grips with the new order. It is in this regard that others have noted the great significance of evangelical religion, with its emphasis upon a dramatic conversion experience, as a powerful tool for social and psychological adaptation. Adolescence increasingly came to be understood as the proper time for such a transformation, and evangelical religion was seen as the appropriate means. The conversion experience, accompanied by the public testimony and the marked changes in personal life associated with it, became an important rite of passage from youth to adulthood, serving in some way both to liberate the individual from his past and to define his new role as a responsible adult. Thus the dominant revivalistic Protestantism of the time was important for many in giving meaning to this process of finding place. [15]

W. Norton, 1972), 483–99. On changes to the institution of apprenticeship, see W. J. Rorabaugh, *The Craft Apprentice: From Franklin to the Machine Age in America* (New York: Oxford University Press, 1986). On the new order, see Paul Johnson, *A Shopkeeper's Millennium: Society and Revivals in Rochester, New York, 1815–1837* (New York: Hill and Wang, 1978).

15. On the general question of youth during this period, see Berthoff, *An Unsettled People;* Oscar and Mary F. Handlin, *Facing Life: Youth and Family in American History* (Boston: Little, Brown, 1971); and Bernard Wishy, *The Child and the Republic: The Dawn of Modern American Child Nurture* (Philadelphia: University of Pennsylvania

Episcopalians of Seabury's stripe, however, rejected this conversion-centered piety on both theological and social grounds, and hence could not avail themselves of this evangelical solution. The young Seabury's challenge involved finding a place in the new order for himself without abandoning the religion of his family. This, by necessity, gave him the task of finding not only a place for *himself* in the new society, but a place for his inherited *religion* as well.

In this endeavor, of course, he was not alone. Many others within his communion were forced to ponder the question of reconciling the new social order with their understanding of God's plan for the world and also, more practically, to determine how to "place" their church in the new milieu. Their struggle to make religious sense of the world was connected with the ramifications of the shift noted earlier from Anglican to Protestant Episcopal. Anglicanism was never the dominant church during the colonial period. Though the church had been established in the southern colonies, in 1770 it included only about 20 percent of the entire colonial population. Yet their self-vision as somehow being a pillar of the social order supplied comfort and meaning. Denied this vision in the early national period, they found themselves only one small denomination among many others in a society that bore little resemblance to the traditional social order. How to make sense of themselves and the new American society became the challenge of the day. One can perhaps call this task the challange of "Americanization" since it involved the responsibility of defining the role of their church in the new American environment, but in the New York in which Seabury lived and

---

Press, 1968). On the particular question of the function of religion for youth coming of age in the early republic, see Lois W. Banner, "Religion and Reform in the Early Republic: the Role of Youth," *American Quarterly* 23 (1971): 677–95; Joseph F. Kett, "Growing Up in Rural New England, 1800–1840," in Tamara K. Hareven, ed., *Anonymous Americans: Explorations in Nineteenth-Century Social History* (Englewood Cliffs, N.J.: Prentice Hall, 1971), 1–16; and Kett, "Adolescence and Youth in Nineteenth-Century America," in Theodore K. Rabb and Robert I. Rotberg, ed., *The Family in History: Interdisciplinary Essays* (New York: Octagon Books, 1976).

worked the result of this "Americanization" was far different from the experience of other religious communities.

In Seabury's orbit of New York Episcopalians the most ambitious religious attempt to work out a new vision of church and society was that offered by John Henry Hobart and his associates. Hobart (1775–1830) was a dominant figure in his day. As a priest and, after 1811, as a bishop, Hobart—through books, sermons, tracts, and broadsides—labored to set forth a place for the Episcopal Church in the new republic that was far different from the old vision of the hierarchical sacred order. Through its revolution America had severed the bond that had linked church and state together since the time of Constantine; hence, he argued, the proper model for the right understanding of the church was no longer that of the established Church of England, but rather the primitive or pre-Constantinian church that had flourished independent of the state. Hobart went further. The loss of establishment was in many ways a good thing—established churches such as the Church of England were often more concerned with undergirding the sacred-social milieu than in maintaining purity in doctrine and order. As Hobart noted, the price of establishment was that a church became encumbered by secular concerns and local pecularities. Now that the church in America was independent, it revered the English tradition only "so far as those principles maintain primitive faith order and worship distinct from secular influence and local arrangements."[16] The American church need not lament its loss of official establishment since it could boast of its fealty to the teachings of the primitive or "pure" church. And the witness of the early church, Hobart and his associates continued, unequivocably testified that bishops were an essential part of the polity of the true church.

Such a witness allowed the newly formed Protestant Episcopal Church to see itself as not simply one religious group among many in nineteenth-century America, but instead as standing apart. "Ap-

16. John Henry Hobart, *The Origin, General Character, and the Present Situation of the Protestant Episcopal Church in the United States of America* (Philadelphia, 1814), 14.

ostolic order" became the battle cry of these individuals; any true church in the present age must still reflect both the order and spirit of the apostolic church. Episcopalians alone among American Protestants could claim an authority in direct historical succession from the church of the apostles. Ordination carried this special gift. Every Episcopal clergyman, no matter how reduced his circumstance, could claim the authority of this eighteen-hundred-year pedigree. The apostolic succession anchored his status both within his congregation and in the greater society. He might be dependent economically upon the laity; his congregation might be small in the world's eyes; yet from the true perspective he stood upon the same rock as did the apostles and saints before him. Finally, since the church itself rested upon this same rock, it should accordingly look backward into its own past to find its definition, not out to the world. Episcopal bishops hence were not portrayed by Hobartians, as they were in England, as part of the order of the greater society. They were likened instead to the patriarchs of the Old Testament, guiding their flock through a desacralized wilderness. This was the theological starting point for young men like Seabury, and it made them wholly out of step with the rest of their Protestant neighbors. His communion may have been a small one, but for Seabury all others would always be simply "dissenters."

Coupled with this emphasis upon the model of the primitive church was the most radical and controversial aspect of the Hobartian understanding: its shrinking of the religious sphere. A chasm separated the concerns of the church from the concerns of the society, a concept which followed as a corollary from the Hobartian vision of the church. The true ecclesiastical model for America was the pre-Constantinian church, which was a pure community surrounded by a hostile world. The church was the vessel of God, the body of Christ; the world, in contrast, had no divinely prescribed social order. No longer did the social order of things reflect God's will and plan as it did for members of the Church of England. The true religious community must always be episcopally governed;

God had made that clear both from revelation in scripture and by the witness of the early church.

The organization of the social realm, however, was ultimately accidental, possessing none of the fixedness of the true church. Society could be monarchical, it could be aristocratic, it could be republican. It could be socially rigid or socially fluid. Whether a given society was any of these or a combination of them was dependent upon external forces (such as geography), or the accidents of history, but never upon the expressed will of God. Individuals then could not expect any explicitly divine directions in the ordering of the proper society.

In suggesting such a different set of rules for church and society the Hobartians were echoing elements already voiced in the pre-Constantinian era, yet in nineteenth-century America the message had a very different effect. In earlier times this church-world dichotomy usually resulted in the conclusion that it was the Christian's responsibility to separate from the world. For the Hobartians it produced an opposite response. Rather than withdrawing, the true believer must continue to respond to the world, but he must do so recognizing that the social order is now desacralized.

In divorcing concerns of the church from those of society the Hobartians trampled upon one of the most cherished principles of the early nineteenth century. Most American Protestants were aghast at the implication that America was a desacralized society. Inspired by a millennial vision of America as God's new Israel and armed with a confidence (particularly strong among Calvinists) that the Bible was as reliable a guide for the good society as for the true church, American Protestant evangelicals saw it as their religious obligation to reformulate society according to God's directive. If America were to be a nation under God, they argued, it must conform to God's law. These evangelicals accordingly dedicated themselves to the great task of missionizing, educating, and reforming America. Through all of these endeavors the Hobartians stood aloofly aside, and at times actively criticized evangelicals for confusing religious issues with social issues. It was not that the Hobartians denied the fact that the nation as well as the church was "under God." If pressed they would gladly have admitted that God was the governor of society as well as of the church, but they would have added that God directed the church through a fixed revelation, while he directed society only by means of common grace, or the general and indirect instruction of the human race manifested in ways such as a reason, prudence, and tradition. The church had no monopoly upon these gifts, and hence spoke with no voice of authority.

There is more than a touch of irony in this disagreement between Hobartians and evangelicals. The spiritual heirs of the colonial Tories became the first religious group in America forced to confront the fact that the social order of America was profane—that is, desacralized—and they did so in the face of an evangelical Protestant opposition which continued instead to see the American society as religious. The disagreement of course stemmed largely from how these two groups would have defined a sacred or truly religious society. As the evangelical position evolved in the early nineteenth century (particularly after the disestablishment of the Congregational Church in Connecticut in 1818) a holy or religious society was one governed by transdenominational principles and directed by the general religious (or, more particularly, Protestant) heritage of moral values. From this perspective America in 1830 was still clearly a religious nation. Indeed this was the genius of the American system. As Robert Baird noted, " '[Christianity] is to this day, though without establishments, and with equal liberty to men's consciences, the religion of the laws and of the government. If records tell the truth . . . our public institutions carry still the stamp of their origin: the memory of better times is come down to us in solid remains; the monuments of the fathers are yet standing; and blessed be God, the national edifice continues visibly to rest upon them.' "[17] Their confi-

17. Robert Baird, *Religion in America* . . . (New York, 1844), 129. Baird is quoting *An Inquiry into the Moral and Religious Character of the American Government,* a work

dence was strengthened even further since many evangelicals could point to the parallels in polity between their churches and the social order. Not until the end of the nineteenth century, when it appeared as if America were being guided by some alien spirit, did evangelicals begin to lose their confidence in the religious foundation of the American order.

The rigid ecclesiology of the Hobartians, in contrast, barred them from any such option. The combination of millennialism and moralism that secured evangelical confidence was for them incomprehensible. A sacred social order would have been an order that reflected the hierarchy and authority of the church. The possibility of such a society was lost forever with the American Revolution, and nothing was going to change this. Christendom was over. This did not mean that Christianity was over, but rather that it was impossible to draw from revelation the answer to the question of how one should live and what one should do in the social realm.

The neat Hobartian distinction between the religious and the social would fall under much criticism by the middle of the nineteenth century. Particularly during the 1850s and 1860s it would be faulted for being ostrichlike in its avoidance of the explosive questions of slavery and secession. Many would damn it for neglecting the historic role of the church as the conscience of the world. Yet, as one sees in Seabury's narrative, this separation of the religious and the social spheres is of tremendous importance in Seabury's coming to peace with himself, his father, his society, his church, and his God. It allowed him to jettison the creaky remains of the old prerevolutionary Tory vision of the sacred order that prevented people like his father from accepting or even comprehending the new social rules of the young republic. By means of the Hobartian dichotomy he was able to be both in his society and true to his religious heritage. By claiming that the church was fixed while society was fluid Hobart

---

usually ascribed to either Theodore Frelinghuysen or Henry Whitings Warner; see Arthur M. Schlesinger, Jr., *The Age of Jackson* (Boston: Little, Brown, 1945), 352.

and his associates were able to transpose the old English religious heritage, thus allowing it to make sense of and ultimately prosper in the open, desacralized American society. It was in many ways a bold action by a group of young clergymen convinced that this was the best way for Episcopalians to adapt to their new society without sacrificing their church's principles. In the course of his memoirs Seabury gropes toward this understanding, which became an important part of his religious confidence in his later ministry.

Themes

Seabury's autobiographical sketch is written in the form of eleven letters or chapters, and the work covers the period between 1814, when Seabury and his family moved from Connecticut to Long Island, and 1821, when he began teaching school in Brooklyn. The work can be subdivided into three major sections. Letters one through five recount his experience in the workshop as an apprentice furniture maker. Letters six through nine treat his elaborate plan of self-education and his attempt to enter upon the world on his own terms. Last, letters ten and eleven describe the religious crisis he underwent between ages eighteen and twenty, and the ultimate resolution of his religious and philosophical questions. As will be seen, however, a number of concurrent themes are intertwined in the narrative.

The first section presents the problem of coming of age and the difficulties of a young man of genteel background yet reduced circumstances in finding an acceptable place in society. The entire story turns on the early decision by Seabury's father to deny his son the opportunity of a classical education and arrange for him instead an appprenticeship with the furniture maker Mr. Moneygripe. On the surface this appeared to be a sensible course of action. Seabury was to follow the great American tale of success, outlined perhaps most famously in the *Autobiography of Benjamin Franklin*, in which a young man, beginning as an apprentice, would rise in the world through a combination of diligence, frugality, and discipline (and more importantly in Franklin's case, the *perception* of these qualities). Cabinetmaking was perhaps the most prestigious and refined of the crafts—requiring much artistic sensitivity—and if pursued vigorously could bring success.[18] Such should have been the result of Seabury's apprenticeship. In fact, for Seabury, the result was pain, frustration, failure, and a tremendous resentment of his father.

What gives this section its poignancy is that, for Seabury, finding a place in society was not merely an economic or social question, but also a psychological and even religious dilemma, underscored by Seabury's ambivalent relationship with his father. The elder Seabury is described as being "indolent" and "devoid of worldly wisdom" yet also as being morally and religiously admirable. Indeed, contemporary accounts of Charles Seabury confirm the latter observation. They praise his otherworldliness and kind disposition. As one writer noted,

> From worldliness I can hardly conceive of one more exempt. *He was too disinterested for the men of this generation. He adhered too faithfully to his baptismal vows to fit his religion to the spirit of the age.* He cherished too sedulously the grace of which his baptism made him a partaker, to fall into the snares which draw so many disciples from consistent allegiance to the Lord . . . . Humble as a little child, he sought only for the authority and sanction of 'thus it is written,' and be the mystery what it may, and be what it may the trial of the pride of the carnal mind, his meek and lowly spirit knew no other sentiment or feeling than 'Speak, Lord, for thy servant heareth.'[19]

18. See, for example, Edward Hazen, *The Panorama of Professions and Trades* . . . (1837; repr. ed., Watkins Glenn, N.Y.: Century House, 1970), 221.

19. Benjamin Tredwell Onderdonk, cited by William B. Sprague, in *Annals of the American Pulpit,* 9 vols. (New York, 1859), 5:402 [first emphasis added]. For a similar assessment of the character of the elder Seabury, see Hallam, *Annals of St. James Church,* 83–84.

Praise such as this, however, is subtly ambiguous, because these virtues are themselves vague. From one perspective the elder Seabury was a saintly individual, eschewing pride and ambition and mirroring the biblical injunction "Be ye not of this world." A life such as his was a silent but subtle rebuke of those around him, since these were virtues that all Christians professed, albeit few fully practiced. Yet from another perspective he was a misfit in the world, constitutionally unable to take charge of his own life, and unwilling to shoulder the responsibilities of father and citizen. He is somewhat reminiscent of the caricature of the guileless parson in literature, such as, for example, Septimus Harding in Anthony Trollope's *Barchester Chronicles*, who is both endearing and frustrating in his other-worldliness. Trollope, however, cushions his parsons from reality by comfortable sinecures in the established church. Charles Seabury was not so lucky.

Seabury's difficult relationship with his father stems from this dilemma. He recognized that his father possessed these virtues of humility, patience, and faithfulness far more than he did himself, and furthermore that they were admirable virtues. Yet, as the younger Seabury noted, "things are stangely out of joint in this world and as Epictetus says every thing here has two handles" (see p. 54, below). The younger Seabury acutely recognized that things were out of joint in this world and that, ironically, his father's very virtues made him unsuitable to the new environment. Charles Seabury's virtues reflected a world still based upon the old Tory sacral vision. The vision may have been reduced politically to shambles by the events of history, but for the elder Seabury it was still the appropriate way in which the true believer was to relate to society. The catechism called him to do his duty in the state of life which it had pleased God to call him, and hence he willfully accepted the depressed condition he found himself in after the Revolution, apparently doing little to try to better either his own state or that of his family. God, for Charles Seabury, was the creator and preserver of the social order, and the only proper human response to that order was humble acceptance. God must know best why he placed people in the station that he did, and hence Charles Seabury could only advise his son, "there is no other way for you but to bear these crosses with patience and to trust that the good providence of God has better times in reserve for you" (see p. 78, below). Because the elder Seabury saw human history as divinely ordered, the picture of him that emerges in the narrative is one of a man puzzled by his son's constant anxiety over his rightful place in the world. For Charles Seabury, his son's place had already been determined by the family's poverty and lack of connections—his son was to become a mechanic, and he must learn to accept his situation. Indeed, several times the elder Seabury actually dissuades his son from reaching beyond his grasp, since it would be ultimately futile and the result would only be dissatisfaction with his present lot.

To accept his lot passively was advice the younger Seabury could not accept. Even in a text written a decade and a half later his anger simmers barely below the surface of his prose and occasionally boils over into it. Yet the anger is also tinged with guilt because Seabury can recognize the higher virtue of his father's advice and admonition, as well as its impracticability. Along with many other things in Epictetus' two handled world, Seabury's father's advice was from one perspective the higher and more virtuous course, yet from another perspective of little value to life as it was lived. The virtues of the elder Seabury were those of an ideal world; the younger Seabury found himself confronting a real world. At times, he would have liked to deny its reality, but he could not, and found himself instead caught between his father's ideals (and by implication his own religious heritage) and his own feelings. He admits, for example, that the reading of romances was usually considered scandalous; nonetheless they stirred within him a vague ambition for something more than his mundane existence.

Similarly, Seabury as narrator can intellectually accept the rightness of his father's belief in the equality of all humans and the dignity of labor, yet his very soul writhes at the smells and sounds of the furniture shop. This tension can especially be seen when he visits with his Aunt Affable and describes his dinners there with the "better sort." He recounts how, during these evenings, he bristled at the condescending remarks and perceived insults and, he confesses, "often have I left her house cursing my miserable lot: and I remember one evening in particular . . . as I was walking down Broadway breaking out into an audible soliloquy—the tears coursing down my cheeks and my voice broken with sobs—'It is Pride—is it? And what if it is pride? Doesn't pride cause as much suffering as any feeling? And doesn't it deserve to be respected?' " (see p. 69, below).

A metaphor that Seabury employs in this section—the bleeding of his pride—is illuminating. It began on the journey to New York City to start his apprenticeship. There he contrasted his own lot with that of a cousin with whom he was staying overnight, who would soon be heading off to Harvard College. Life in the workshop continued to wound it. The final blow came when he accepted a dollar from his master Moneygripe, who had earlier grossly offended his feelings at the time of his mother's death. Pride, according to the teachings of traditional theologians, was the greatest of sins and the source of many lesser sins. Yet for Seabury it was also like blood, the source of life. He painfully acknowledges that without it he simply cannot live happily. This, ultimately, is why Seabury cannot accept the workshop. It is not that it is evil. He (as narrator) willingly acknowledges that the apprentices on the whole were decent human beings, and that even Moneygripe himself was not the ogre whom his memory seemed to picture, yet nonetheless that was how they appeared to him at the time, and that fact could not be denied. He did not fit in because there was for him a reality greater than that of economic circumstance, and that was character. Character for Seabury was shaped by a variety of factors: background, education, as well as the cumulative effect of all previous experience. Character in turn shaped the individual, making him who he was, and he was not malleable enough to adapt comfortably to any or all circumstances. To ignore character was to ignore the most fundamental reality of human nature. Seabury could deny neither who he was, nor that he did not fit in to the world of the workshop.

The tension between what ought to be and what is in fact the case is reflected in the text by one final point of contrast between the older Seabury and the younger. Reflecting on his time as an apprentice Seabury observes,

> In theory every allotment of life may be borne with a reasonable degree of contentment and sufficient incentives will be found in strictly Christian motives to better our outward circumstances and to turn the circumstances themselves to the improvement of our minds. But in fact the case, even with good men, has been otherwise. It is discontent with one condition of life that leads us to aspire to another: and when once we have embarked upon our own course it is pride, ambition or vanity that fills our sails and speeds us on our way. [Pages 67–68, below]

Pride, ambition and vanity, or in other words aspects of unredeemed human nature, were the forces that led individuals to challenge the course of events. The virtuous elder Seabury was humble not proud, content not ambitious, and modest not vain. He also did nothing to better his circumstance. The younger Seabury lacked his father's simplicity and suffered from pride, ambition, and vanity. He also used them to propel him in his search for a place in the world.

The second section of the narrative, letters six through nine, follow Seabury's activities after he leaves Moneygripe and in particular in his determining of what path to follow to find his fortune. After a short, humorous account of his failure at surveying, most of the section treats the reawakening of Seabury's love of learning and his desire to acquire a command of the classical languages. The modern reader will probably be puzzled at the amount of concern Seabury extended in this regard and the excitement he expresses at each stage of his accomplishment. Yet it must be remembered that in 1817 Latin and Greek, far from being dead languages, were still passports to the land of the learned. As Seabury noted in the first part of his story, his father's discouraging of him from learning Latin had relegated him in his schooling to the great unwashed, in contrast to those select few students preparing for college. Whatever learned profession Seabury might have considered, the classical languages were a *sine qua non*. They were to the early 1800s what computer literacy has become to the late 1980s—a necessity for any upward advancement. Thus every lesson Seabury mastered, every book he acquired, every passage of Virgil he translated, seemed to him one more step in finding his way.

In this section of the work the reader senses a noticeable shift in Seabury's tone. Gone is the heaviness and pain of the workshop, with its continued bleeding of the young man's pride, and in its place is a sense of excitement and hope. All of his accomplishments are seen as victories over blind circumstance. The human will *can* triumph over tribulation. The joy of learning and the confidence in his own progress even allow for a sense of playfulness in certain sections of the narrative, most particularly in his account of acquiring a Latin dictionary from the "alchymyst" Eddard. Learning and teaching begin to heal the pride so wounded by Moneygripe. The classics especially are valued because they teach what human beings are and what they might become. He seems to take particular satisfaction that the very dollar he accepted from Moneygripe at the nadir of his apprenticeship—the cruelest blow the workshop was to level against his pride—was later used to buy his first Latin text. In another place Seabury offers a more detailed explanation of the value of the classics:

The ancient languages have been proved to be among the most practical branches of education. They deal not in abstract truth. They supply the mind with a furniture, which, on all subjects of social life, is a valuable help; on many of the most important, an indispensable qualification for clearness of thought and language. They afford proofs and illustrations, not otherwise attainable, of the progress of opinion and the arts. They throw much light, not otherwise discernible, on the nature and diversities of human sentiment. They imbody [*sic*] many singular phenomena, not otherwise discoverable, in the philosophy of mind. . . . They are thus the means of familiarizing the pupil with the scenes of actual life and enriching his mind with the lessons of experience.[20]

If, however, Seabury had in some way reached peace with himself he had still not come to peace with the world. In this section he still seems out of place and ill at ease. Nor does he appear to have reached any religious understanding. He continues to profess the religious faith of his father, and the text suggests that he attends church, yet religious issues seem to drop from the picture. Even though his expressed purpose in acquiring the classical languages was eventually to enter the ministry, Seabury in these chapters is strangely silent on religious questions. Perhaps this is so because in rejecting the counsel of his father in order to secure a place for himself in the world he had discovered the incompatability between his familial faith and the new social circumstance. The result was that his religion lost its integrative power; it no longer made sense of the world. Thus the second section of the work ends with a refusal of a scholarship that would have allowed him to prepare for the ministry.

The last section returns to some of the themes of the first part, and in particular the question of finding one's place. Yet here the question is raised not as a psychological issue but as a philosophical one. What does free will mean in the light of divine providence? Indeed, even if the human will is free, what can be accomplished with it if all else is fixed by fate? As he reflected, "In relation to these great events [that is, those things determined by fate] our individual wills are the winds in the cavern of Aeolus; our energies may struggle and our passions roar: they will but rage around the barriers of determinate counsel while the Supreme Ruler restrains them with authority and

20. Samuel Seabury, *The Study of the Classics on Christian Principles* (Flushing, N.Y., 1831), 3–4.

binds them with the chains and in the prison of destiny" (see pages 113–14, below). But conversely, if the universe is free must it then not be godless since it would lose all marks of providence? Upon the right answer to these questions Seabury's future rested, since what lay at stake was either his hard won freedom or his familial faith. These questions make the focus of the last part of the work far different from those that preceeded it. Autobiographical events are largely subordinated to the question of human freedom and the right religious vision of the universe. How can the universe be big enough, Seabury asks, to include an all-powerful God and free human beings?

To answer this question Seabury, mirroring in many ways the similar movement by the Hobartians, works towards a new view of providence markedly different from that assumed by his father. God's providence vis-à-vis humanity lay not in his creating and fixing of all things (which by implication would make any challenge to the order of things blasphemous) but rather in his general guidance and direction of human beings. Throughout the memoirs Seabury makes use of the image of the sailboat to describe the human predicament. God's providence is likened to the wind that can move us if we allow it. The wind may give movement and a general direction but it cannot steer the vessel; that is the human responsibility. God's providence in human life also gives movement but not a set course. It is part of the human predicament to have to choose just as it is part of the responsibility of the navigator to navigate. The openness of the universe, far from being contrary to God's plan, is now understood as part of its essence. God, for Seabury, is within the choice but does not compel the choice.

Seabury reaches this conclusion after wrestling with a number of challenges, but most directly in answering the question of which direction his own religious life should proceed along: toward Roman Catholicism, toward Deism, or back to the church of his fathers. The choice may strike the modern reader as odd, but in the popular Protestant imagination of the early nineteenth century Rome and

Editor's Introduction

Deism were the Scylla and Charybdis of religion. One was the fruit of an excess of sacramentalism, sacerdotalism, and superstition while the other, the opposite extreme, cast off all revealed religion. Yet in practice one extreme could lead to the other, as the life of the great historian Edward Gibbon attested. In his youth, Gibbon had converted to Roman Catholicism and after abandoning it spent the rest of his life attacking revealed religion, most especially in his *Decline and Fall of the Roman Empire*. For Seabury, Roman Catholicism was strange, passionate, exotic and vaguely dangerous. It was a communion in which one could lavish the emotions with symbol and sacrament, ritual and romance. This part of Rome's appeal would lead Seabury and others later in the century to kindle some of this same ritual and sacramentalism within their own communion. Yet Seabury did not make the decision to embrace Rome, just as he did not ultimately accept the materialism of his Deist companion, though it did lead him into a spiral of doubts and made him for a time lose confidence in any divine providence. Rather he ended with a renewed confidence in Protestant (Episcopal) Christianity as set forth by such exponents of natural theology and the evidences of Christianity as William Paley, Joseph Butler, and Thomas Chalmers.

A sense of disappointment perhaps befalls the modern reader, though. After such an exciting tale why return to a mundane solution served up by authors generally considered as making up the nadir of Christian apologetics—writers who simultaneously combine the worst qualities of evangelicalism, rationalism, and British academic writing? Yet as one sees in the case of Seabury, the apologists were successful among those who in the early nineteenth century struggled with belief because so many of these individuals *wanted* a reason to believe. For Seabury, Paley, Butler, and the others gave evidence not simply for the creation of the world but for "Parental affection, filial duty, conjugal fidelity, honesty, gratitude, [and] all that dignify the species and endear them to one another" (see p. 133, below). For Seabury, as perhaps for many more in his generation, the choice was not a disinterested weighing of conflicting arguments, but rather that between two starkly different pictures of the universe—one dark and empty and the other filled with all of the affections noted above. One look into the abyss of the materialistic universe brought Seabury back into the warm glow of the familiar.

Yet one should carefully note how the dicussion ends: with the question, that if all of the above were true, why was there only *probable* evidence and not positive proof? The reason, for Seabury, was because at its core the universe, just as society, involved choice. God providentially offered only probable evidence because our response had to be a decision of character. Human responsibility was necessary on all levels of existence. Man lives in an "open universe" just as he lives in an open society. The openness in no way guaranteed either that all would believe or that all would socially rise. Both remained tests of character. But it *could* be done, and indeed it was one's duty to try. Seabury rejected finally the indifferent passivity and waiting upon God that characterized his father, and replaced it with the responsibility of human choice. God in all cases would provide help, but never overwhelming help. That was the human predicament.

Hence Seabury was being both true and equivocating when he ended his work with a final nautical image, "Let me rather be thankful that after roaming over the waters of the great abyss I had strength given me to return into the ark from which I had flown" (see p. 134, below). In a sense Seabury did return home. His later career would see him following in his father's footsteps—entering the ministry and having a fruitful and distinguished career. Yet picking up the question by its "other handle" Seabury ended quite differently from where he had started. He began by wrestling with the dilemma of confronting the new American society armed only with the social and religious heritage of his Tory father. The inevitable result was a tremendous tension between ideal and reality. He ended at peace with himself, his society, and his God. That peace, however, was only brought about by jettisoning the passive providence that undergird his father's cosmos and accepting the responsibility of a dynamic providence. In this regard he would join with many young Hobartians in continuing the words of the old religion but singing them to a very different tune.

Literary Influences

Seabury's writing is marked with the flourish and élan of a self-educated individual. Proud of his learning and wit he is not averse to sharing his hard-won erudition with his readers. He cites texts from memory, drops classical allusions, and writes in a generally elevated tone. Furthermore, he clearly has literary pretensions in the organization and structure of his narrative. In the story of his coming of age his writing never assumes the tone of a simple recounting of events, instead it bears the distinct echo of some of Seabury's early reading.

Early in the work Seabury describes his devotion to such picaresque novels as René Le Sage's *The Adventures of Gil Blas* and Tobias Smollet's *The Adventures of Roderick Random*. As he notes these works "enriched my mind with a wide variety of materials by which I enlarged my knowledge of human nature and gained considerable facility in the discrimination of character" (see pp. 53–54, below). Both are tales of the adventures of young men coming of age, and their influence may have shaped both the way in which Seabury structures his narrative, as well as the tone he assumes in certain sections. The rapid episodic structure Seabury employs in telling his story may also partly reflect his childhood reading. One adventure follows another in quick succession giving the narrative a quality of impatience and restlessness. Furthermore, like Gil Blas and Roderick Random, Seabury has the tendency to see himself as an outsider, cut off from comfort and support. Blas and Random were physically alienated from their environment, while Seabury felt psychologically isolated, but in both the case of Seabury's narrative and that of his childhood favorites the narrator is forced to rely upon his own resources for his survival in a world that does not quite make sense.[21]

Another aspect of Seabury's style reminiscent of the picaresque tradition is his ample mixing of humor with the pathos of his story. The pseudonyms which he chooses for his characters—Moneygripe for his parsimonious employer, Alf Hothead for one excitable apprentice and Ike Redface for another brandy-imbibing one, Aunt Affable for his socially prominent relative, and Dr. Rubric for the pretentious clergyman—all manifest a farcical spirit. The world may be out of sorts, but the best response may be to laugh at it. Indeed some of the episodes such as those concerning the surveyer Mr. Saxon and Eddard the alchemist seem to be almost completely episodes of humor. Seabury has a fine comic touch and in his descriptions of characters creates vivid images. Throughout his narrative he mixes humor and serious purpose in a way reminiscent of that described in the introduction to *Gil Blas*. In it Le Sage tells a story of two scholars on a road who noticed a stone inscribed "here lies interred the soul of the licentiate Peter Garcias." One scholar thought such an inscription foolish, since souls cannot be interred, and dismissed it. The other found the inscription a puzzle, and began digging under the stone only to find out that the interred "soul" turned out to be a purse full of money. Le Sage concludes, "No matter who you are, you must be like one or the other of these two students. If you cast your eye over my adventures without fixing it on the moral concealed under them, you will derive very little benefit from the perusal: but if you read with attention you will find that mixture of the useful with the agreeable, so successfully prescribed by Horace."[22] To mingle the useful and the agreeable also seems to be Seabury's concern.

21. Robert Alter, *Roque's Progress: Studies in the Picaresque Novel* (Cambridge, Mass.: Harvard University Press, 1964), 1–34.
22. [Alain] René Le Sage, *The Adventures of Gil Blas of Santillane,* trans. Tobias Smollett, 3 vols. (London, N.D.), 1: vii–viii.

Editor's Introduction

As many echoes of his early love of the picaresque as one finds in Seabury's narrative, it departs from the genre in at least two important ways. Unlike Random and Blas, Seabury is not a rogue. At the center of his story is not a happy-go-lucky rascal, by no means averse to bending the law whenever it might suit him, but a confused yet sincere young man trying to find himself in the world. Hence the point of the story is not simply to recount the adventures, as with a true picaresque tale, but instead to show how the problems that set him apart from his family, society, and God were finally dealt with. His is a story of growth rather than a mere series of adventures.

Seabury's sketch also has great value as a historical document. He opens a window into the everyday world of New York in the early nineteenth century. He was, of course, by no means a disinterested observer—his narrative at times burns with a passion—but his distinct vantage point as an individual straddling the worlds of the drawing room and the workshop gives to his observations keen insight. His narrative uniquely provides, for example, both a glimpse of life among the apprentices and also how this world appeared to one reared in a more genteel environment.

Seabury offers a vivid picture of the intricacies of social relationships in the young republic. The pains and affronts to pride he recounts remind the reader that class distinctions were far from eliminated. Seabury's sensitive nature made him constantly aware of questions of status and social standing and hence his narrative offers insight into the relative status of teachers, clergy, surveyers, and the other occupations he encounters. This is particularly true in that part of the tale concerning his apprenticeship. Seabury's father might have believed that apprenticeship was a step toward advancement, just as it had been at the time of Benjamin Franklin, yet Seabury's description of his world presents a very different perception. His narrative relates two seemingly insignificant incidents, that nevertheless pointedly bear witness to the low status of apprentices and their relationship to the genteel community. At his first meal at Moneygripe's Seabury was affronted that the apprentices were not only fed from the remains of the master's table but also fed along with the maids, since it seemed to reflect the servile position in which the apprentices were held. The second incident involved the question of his accepting of gratuities for delivering furniture to genteel customers. Clearly for Seabury to accept a gratuity, like a common porter, would have been a sign of deference and a further confirmation of his (new) servile status. These and other such details cast light upon the changing social relationships of the early national period.

Through Seabury's eyes the reader can also learn much about the work and social habits of apprentices in what was still a largely preindustrial artisan culture. He describes in detail their responsibilities and daily work routines, as well as painting a picture of everyday life in the garret. In his account the sights and smells come alive. Seabury's workplace had not yet been touched by the forces of the temperance movement, and hence his account includes descriptions of the celebrations for the coming of a journeyman and other drinking patterns of the apprentices. One also sees how the apprentices viewed religion before the forces of the Second Great Awakening were felt. Despite the public piety of Moneygripe the apprentices were left to themselves in matters of religion and Deism, and free thinking still largely ruled "below the stairs."

Finally, Seabury's account is of value to the student of the history of American education. From his description of the usher's role of making pens and ruling copybooks to his detailed accounts of courses and texts, Seabury provides a series of vignettes of education in the early American republic. His care in describing the continuing role of classical education in this period will be of great interest to educational historians.

A Note on the Text

The only copy of Seabury's autobiographical sketch known to be extant is that found in the Seabury Family Papers in the New-York

Historical Society, and this transcription is based upon it. It is contained on 106 closely written pages of manuscript and is remarkably legible. Seabury's hand is surprisingly clear for one who proclaimed in the work a detestation for "every attempt to use the pen with mechanical precision" (pp. 116–17, below). Only in a few places is the text indecipherable.

The title page of the manuscript reads, "Autobiographical Sketch—written in 1831—brought down to 1820–1—with memoranda made after talking with him in 1861 and 1864 and at other times by WmJS." This notation suggests why there are three distinct handwritings in the work. The title page is undoubtedly the work of William J. Seabury, son of Samuel (III). A second hand, which wrote the body of the text, was Seabury's own, circa 1831. Finally, there are a few corrections to the text (including the request that it be burnt) made by a third and far less steady hand. This last, in all likelihood, was that of Seabury reviewing his own memoirs in the 1860s.

As it exists the manuscript is clearly a penultimate draft. Seabury was a careful literary craftsman in his published works and the present version of his narrative has an unfinished sense about it. This factor has affected my editorial approach to the text. Where the text shows evidence of authorial correction, whether by cancellation or interlineation, I have accepted the edited reading; where a change has been significant, though, I discussed it in the footnotes. In a few places where he seems to have inadvertently left out a key word from a sentence, thus rendering it incomprehensible, I have felt obliged to suggest within brackets an approximation of the word intended. Furthermore, I have followed the rule that all abbreviations should be expanded to the degree that Seabury himself would have done so. He regularly made use of a not-always-consistent form of shorthand abbreviations, and these too have been expanded—for example, *ing* for "g," *Christianity* for "Xnty," *with* for "w.," *which* for "wh.," and the spelling out of all ampersands. Numerical references have also been spelled out. Furthermore, quotation marks have been added to all dialogue in the text, and an occasional comma has been quietly added for the sake of the modern reader. In one or two places I have seen fit to add parentheses for clarity, but these are always bracketed. I have also regularized and spelled out the chapter headings. Following the practice common to Seabury's time, however, Latin phrases are left unitalicized except when explicitly emphasized by the author. Translations are taken, when possible, from *The Loeb Classics Library* editions.

Seabury, as has been noted, was proud of his hard-won education and took great relish in his vocabulary. Occasionally, however, he seems to create his own words, and where he does so has been noted. Spelling has not been regularized, and Seabury will occasionally be found using both American and British spellings of certain words. All of these editorial decisions have been made out of a concern for making the text as accessible as possible to the modern reader while in no way sacrificing its integrity.

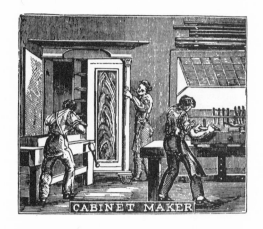

PART TWO

The Letters

One

Sept. 5th 1831

My dear friend,

In compliance with your request I undertake to spread on paper some particulars of a life to the outlines of which you have often heard me refer in conversation and which you were pleased to think might be useful to others if generally known. I begin without any previous reflection and quite in doubt whether I shall find it worthwhile to proceed beyond the first letter. For though Dr. Johnson has said that the story of every man's life might be made an instructive biography, yet I cannot help thinking that in most cases this could only be accomplished by talents somewhat similar to those of the great moralist himself.[1]

My father at and some years after the time of my birth was the minister of the Episcopal Society at [New London].[2] He is a man of many excellent endowments of mind but it is only necessary for my present purpose to remark that his intellectual powers were of a moderate grade and considering his station in society far from being highly cultivated—at least in all academical branches of education. He was without property, dependent on a small salary for the support of a wife and five children,—of an indolent disposition totally inconsistent with energy of character, and absolutely devoid of that

1. Dr. Johnson made this observation in the *Idler*, no. 84. It is alluded to by James Boswell in the beginning of *The Life of Samuel Johnson LL.D.* (New York: The Modern Library, n.d.), 7.

2. At a number of places in the text Seabury was purposely vague as to particulars, no doubt because many of the persons to whom he referred were still alive in 1831. Where I have been able to supply the information with certainty I have included it in brackets within the body of the text. In those instances where there is only probable evidence I discuss it in a footnote.

worldy wisdom—which in many cases is to be found to be an ample substitute for worldly property. But lest what I have thus felt myself obliged to say may give you an unfavourable impression of my father, allow me to add that in all that constitutes moral and religious worth—I have never known a better man. His piety is inobtrusive but sincere. His integrity is inflexible. He overflows with the milk of human kindness. He has great good humor, a readiness of wit, and can always introduce an appropriate anecdote with much innocent playfulness. And though few men would be less likely to arrive at sound conclusions by a process of logical deduction yet no man I know of is so well spared the need of such a course by possessing an instinctive shrewdness that guides him straight in the common matters of life and gives him a wonderful facility in estimating the character of those around him.

My mother was a woman of a character in many respects opposite. She possessed an acute sensibility which rendered her, even on the ordinary topics and incidents of life, keenly alive to the transports of joy and sorrow. Never did [a] woman cherish for her family a more devoted attachment and I believe I may safely add that maternal anxiety has not often been reciprocated with a truer filial affection. Sensibility was the point of her character: and I need not dwell on its other features further than to remark that she was a woman of a mind naturally good and as well cultivated as was consistent with the due discharge of those domestic duties to which her life was devoted. She possessed an amiable piety which she endeavored by every means in her power to transfuse into the bosoms of her children. Her constitution was feeble and ever since my remembrance she was the victim of ill health.

In what light I was regarded by others as a boy I cannot say but I well remember that I used to think myself rather dull and backward. I had very little of that self confidence which gives to many children a prepossessing air of smartness. I was ambitious but from a native timidity was easily dashed and hence utterly unfitted to take the lead in our boyish pursuits. Courage was certainly not the most prominent feature of my mind and the little stock I had was far from being increased by the daily lectures I received on the merits of patience and submissiveness, and the great sinfulness of resentment and retaliation. On the whole, though few boys would make greater sacrifice for their sport, yet I felt that my best standing was at school and it is no wonder therefore if I was somewhat partial to its exercises. Here I was generally with two or three more a competitor for the head of my class and had often the satisfaction of enjoying a triumph over those who perhaps within an hour after would convince me by a kick or a cuff or some similar *ad hominem* argument that *la morale* and *la physique* were dispensed in rather different proportions.

As I wish to render my narrative as brief as possible I will merely observe that I was kept at the ordinary day schools of the village until I was between eleven and twelve years of age—at which time I was transferred to another of recent standing [and] of somewhat higher grade. At the former schools my studies were reading, writing, and arithmetic and at the latter they were increased by the addition of English Grammar and Geography including as was said the use of the globes—which consisted by the bye, chiefly in being taught to solve the wonderful problem of discovering the time of day in any part of the earth with no other *data* than were afforded by the old town clock of the village. This last school was called a classical school: that is to say—a school in which some half dozen boys who were *fitting for college* monopolized by far the greater portion of the time and attention of the Instructor to the great detriment of about thirty others who had a fair prospect of going unfitted into the world.[3] I once came very near being enrolled among these envied few for so I used to consider them. My father indeed had no intention of sending me to college and he was utterly averse to having me initiated into the mysteries of the Latin tongue, but my entreaties had once so far overcome his resolution that he permitted me to take from his library an old Latin grammar in order to join a class that was

3. Seabury is here describing a mixed school in which both an English and a Latin curriculum were taught.

then about forming for a study that has to most minds so little that is alluring. He accompanied the permission, however, with so many assurances of the futility and difficulties of the pursuit and with such earnest persuasion that I would give my attention to things of which would prove to be of more benefit to me that I reluctantly replaced the volume and had soon the mortification of finding boys with whom I had ranked equally in other branches advanced as I thought far ahead of me by the fluency with which they could repeat the inflections of *Dominus* and roll out the learned jargon of *hic, haec, hoc*.

So far from attaching any blame to my father's [?] for this course of procedure in this respect I would rather recommend his conduct as worthy of imitation. His circumstances did not permit him to bestow on his sons a liberal education. He knew the state of dependence and mortifying disappointment which a superficial preparation could scarcely fail to entail on a professional life. He was aware of the dangers which the counting house or the store offered to those who had neither friends nor capital to promise them advancement. He despised and dreaded above all things the character of an idle gentleman. He deprecated the forwardness so generally manifested by parents to press their children into the ranks of doctors, lawyers, ministers, and merchants without much regard for their fitness for any of these stations, and he determined himself to bring up his children as *mechanics* in which capacity he thought they would have the least temptation to forfeit the virtues of sobriety and honesty and stand the best chance to reap the advantages of frugal and industrious habits. How far correct he was in this determination I shall have occasion to consider in a future letter. But certainly with this prospect in view the exclusion of the dead languages in the education of his children was highly judicious. There were other subjects to which their time could be more profitably devoted; and any respectable proficiency in what is strictly termed *learning* could only serve to raise them above their humble destination or render them, when placed in it, vain and conceited.

As this was the school at which my education, so far as it was entrusted to others, was finished. I may be permitted to state my recollections with some particularity. I had not the remotest idea that I was a *smart* boy—conceiving this character to be monopolized by those that studied Latin and went to college. And yet from what I can remember I think I must have been tolerably apt in the studies which I pursued. As for teaching, even in this, by far the best school which I attended, it was miserably defective—indeed it could hardly be said to exist at all. There were maps and globes and from those I acquired a pretty good stock of Geographical knowledge. My knowledge of Arithmetic was something like a merchant's property of two kind—paper and cash—real and apparent. I had ciphered three times through Daboll's Arithmetic and could work out the hardest questions it contained.[4] I had gone through the treatise on Arithmetic in the first volume of Webber's Mathematics[5] and had learned how to make traverse tables and use logarithms in Flint's Surveying.[6] Of course my *nominal* capital for a boy of twelve years was very decent—and it was with no little chagrin that I was a few years afterwards compelled to admit that whatever facilities I might have acquired in the mysteries of the *art* of Arithmetic I was almost totally destitute of any acquaintance with its principles as a Science. Indeed it could not be otherwise where knowledge was gained not in consequence of the *Preceptor's* aptness to *teach* but of the *pupil's* aptness to *imitate*. Alegbra was understood to be reserved for the privileged inmates of the college and I knew of it only by name. Declamation was a stated exercise of the school and I among others was compelled to take my share in it. I always avoided it if I could; for though ambitious to excel yet an excessive bashfulness and awkwardness of manner and a thickness of utterance—defects that could

4. Nathan Daboll (1750–1818), *Daboll's Schoolmaster's Assistant. Being a Plain Practical System of Arithmetic. . . .* (first edition, 1800).

5. Samuel Webber (1759–1810), comp., *Mathematics Compiled from the Best Authors and Intended to be the Text-Book of the Course of Private Lectures on these Sciences in the University at Cambridge* (1801).

6. Abel Flint (1765–1825), *A System of Geometry and Trigonometry; Together with a Treatise on Surveying. . . .* Flint's work was printed in America through 1850.

only be overcome by more pains and skill than it has ever been my fortune to have the benefit of—exposed me generally to disappointment and not infrequently to ridicule.

Before I leave this period of my story let me remark that I possessed at this time two acquirements without which I could not have a [*sic*] taken a single step of my subsequent advancement. The one of these was the ability to spell correctly and to read fluently. The other was the ability to parse, as it is termed, an English sentence and apply to its construction the rules of Syntax. For the former of these I am indebted to a faithful old woman—now deceased—who taught me before I was seven years of age and who thus conferred on me an obligation which I shall always remember with gratitude but can never requite. For the latter—which I acquired at the last school I attended—I must make my acknowledgement not to the teacher but to a patient plodding boy who had had the subject for the two preceding years under the regular compression of his thumb and finger and to whom, my teacher under the pressure of other and more important engagements, referred me for initiation. I soon became familiarized to the mechanical process by which boys are familiarized to parcel off nouns and verbs and class their several accidents—and such rapid progress did I make that, to the great surprise of my young aid, I could stand my part of the drilling without once referring to the dictionary to ascertain the parts of speech. Absolutely mechanical as this process was it was yet of essential use to me. It gave me information which proved, to me at least, the key of the literary world and which I do not believe I should ever otherwise have obtained. I was soon brought to see that the rules of Murray's Grammar[7] which I could easily repeat from memory—instead of being as it always appeared a mass of consummate nonsense was a compendium of valuable truth. I never until some years after saw a book that pretended to give the subject an analytical dress—the only

7. Lindley Murray (1745–1826), *English Grammar, Adapted to the Different Classes of Learners* . . . (first edition, 1795). According to the D. N. B., Murray's Grammar "monopolized the field" during the first half of the nineteenth century.

one which is intelligible to beginners—and for this reason I think that had I not learned to parse at the time I did I should never have understood the grammatical structure of a sentence. Such attainments, therefore as I may at present possess in English literature or in Latin or Greek I attribute to the happy circumstance which opened to me the mysteries of English Grammar. And I cannot forbear to remark, as an instance of the influence of early impressions on subsequent opinions that the pleasure which I dervied in discovering as I gradually did the full meaning of the definitions, etc., in Murray's Abridgement with which my memory was stored strongly prepossessed my mind with a preference for the synthetic over the analytical mode of instruction.[8]

8. Synthetic learning involves learning through observation and experience before mastering the theory behind the rules.

Two

To this small stock of school knowledge I could add but little from the stores of miscellaneous reading. The first volume of Echard's Roman History[1] which I had read three times—the abridgement of Greece and England by Goldsmith[2] and the first volume of Roderick Random[3] are—if not all the books which I had read—at least those which had left on my mind the deepest impressions. Some other books—particularly poetry—I had read for the credit of the act but these I had read for my enjoyment. Thus furnished I quitted the place of my nativity [New London, Connecticut] on the eleventh of July 1814 having on the preceding month completed my thirteenth year. We sailed under the protection of a passport from the Commander of the British squadron which at that time had possession of the [Long Island] Sound.[4] In consequence of bad weather we had put into the mouth of the Conn[ecticut River]. Next morning we left the harbor in company with several other small craft that had been detained from a similar cause. By the time we were well out in the Sound we observed a couple of small barges making toward us. On the night before a British midshipman with two or three men had been surprised and made prisoners and these barges we conjectured—rightly

1. Laurence Echard (1670–1730), *The Roman History, from the Building of the City* . . . [*to the Taking of Constantinople by the Turks*]. Many editions.

2. Oliver Goldsmith (1728–74). His *History of England from Earliest Times to the Death of George II* and *The History of Greece from the Earliest State to the Death of Alexander the Great* were both regularly abridged for school use.

3. Like other picaresque novels, *The Adventures of Roderick Random*, written in 1748 by Tobias Smollett, is concerned with the adventures of a young man in quest of fame and fortune.

4. Seabury's allusion here is to the activity of the British navy off the coast of New England during the last months of the War of 1812.

as it afterward seemed—were repairing to the scene of action with the view to recover, if possible, their loss. Alarmed at the sight of the enemy all the other vessels in our company to the number of about twenty put back while we, secure in our passport, continued our course. But no sooner was it found that we were proceeding on our way alone than we became an object of suspicion. Forgetting or perhaps not aware of the circumstance that his commanding officer had granted a permit to a clergyman to transport his family and furniture through the Sound the commander of the barges could no otherwise account for our apparent boldness in pushing fearlessly ahead than the conjecture that armed men were concealed in our hold. After eying us therefore for some time at a respectful distance he concluded that it was most safe to retire and abandon the object of his pursuit—vowing vengence at the same time against the craft that had ventured to interrupt him. He therefore rowed off in the direction of the squadron and was soon out of sight. This was about nine o'clock A.M. At four P.M. we discovered four barges of a larger size making steadily towards us. We had no wind and they soon overtook us and boarded us. In an instant a party of gruff looking fellows powered in upon either quarter and through the cabin windows. Some of us were a little agitated at this strange scene—my mother however sat on the quarter deck and was so little moved by the incident as to feel inclined—had not my father begged her to be silent—to rally the lieutenant on the valor of his soldiers in breaking some of her crockery in their forcible entry. But imagine the disappointment of the officer himself when he found the hold filled not with armed men—but with the goods and chattels of a country parson! He behaved however very handsomely: regretted his mistake, drank a glass of wine and suffered us to continue our course unmolested.

Within a day or two we arrived at [Caroline Church in Setauket, Long Island] the place of our destination and within a few days were comfortably settled in our new residence. The people of the place were farmers of the plainest kind—illiterate and uncultivated and we were therefore thrown into very different society from that which we had left. For my own part I was thrown upon myself with little or nothing to do. To go to school in the village was out of the question—as the very fact of my having been to school all my life time—summer as well as winter—constituted me a sort of prodigy of learning in the estimation of the natives—who after hearing me recount my accomplishments concluded I had left nothing more to be learned.[5] My father finding that his boys were running wild and that it was impossible for him to keep them employed at home was induced to comply with the request of the villagers and take charge of their school himself. It thus became my province to hear the young urchins their *b–a*–ba[6] and show the largest how to perform the more difficult questions of their arithmetic; thus relieving my father of the two extremes of his juvenile cure for both of which he had an equally strong aversion—the one being as repugnant to the indolence of his mind as was the other to his love of bodily ease. This project was of short duration: my father becoming disgusted with the impertinent interference of his dignified patrons—one of whom, I remember, was loud in her complaints that her Betsey was heard only twice in the morning (there were about sixty scholars) whereas Mr. Snapjack the former teacher used to hear her four times. This important institution being dissolved I was again left to run at large. I used to amuse myself by joining the farmers at their work and frequently going into the woods with them by which half a day at least was consumed. While at home a considerable portion of my time was devoted to reading: some of it of a profitable kind. Several articles on biography and similar subjects in the N. Ed. Encyclope-

5. This reaction reflected the varying levels of public education in the different states. Like other New Englanders, citizens of Connecticut regularly boasted of their fine public education system, which was lacking at the time in New York. See Timothy Dwight, *Travels in New England and New York*, 4 vols. (Cambridge, Mass.: Harvard University Press, 1969), 4:206–17.

6. Seabury here is citing an example of the most elementary level of syllabary teaching (syllable construction), a method of instruction still used at the time.

dia[7] were of lasting benefit to me. At this time too I formed acquaintance with Don Quixote and Sancho Panza and they became my
favorite companions.[8] But the chief of my reading was the most
useless and mischievous of all reading—the tales and romances of
periodical journals two or three volumes of which were to be found
among my father's books. Occasionally at my mother's instigation I
attempted some serious studies. Twice I remember sitting down to a
venerable translation of Euclid—but having no one to assist and little
to encourage me the *pons asinorum*[9]—to my shame be it said!—was
exchanged for the more attractive pages of some idle novel. Thus I
continued to live for about fifteen months of the most valuable
portion of my life. I was under no discipline—no regular study. Yet
the time was not wholly wasted—on the contrary I am sensible to
this day of its favorable influence on my character. The Encyclopedia
gave me much useful information and tended in a small degree to
consolidate my mind. Don Quixote cherished a taste for wit and
furnished me with many apt allusions. The novels and romances of
the love sick order though they tended to enfeeble the mind and
inspirit it with visionary expectations, at the same time excited and
warmed the feelings and infused into my bosom a vague ambition
which was ready to serve in the first definite object that presented
itself. Nor ought I to omit to mention that Gil Blas[10] and Roderick
Random (of the former of which I was passionately fond) enriched
my mind with a variety of materials by which I enlarged my knowl-

7. Seabury here may be referring to the then popular *New and Complete American Encyclopaedia*, published in New York between 1805 and 1811.

8. *The Adventures of Don Quixote de La Mancha*, the novel by Miguel de Cervantes, is but another of the works of a picaresque flavor that amused the young Seabury and quite probably helped him form the structure of the narrative.

9. A Latin phrase literally meaning the ass's bridge. It generally refers to a critical test of ability imposed upon an inexperienced student, and often more particularly referred to the fifth proposition of book one of Euclid, which was regarded as the first difficult theorem that poor students usually stumbled over. This is but the first of many examples where the self-educated Seabury indirectly flaunts his learning.

10. *The Adventures of Gil Blas of Santillane*, cited in the Introduction, note 22, above.

edge of human nature and gained considerable facility in the discrimination of character. These results ought perhaps in a degree to reconcile me to the deprivation of a more regular discipline; for though
it would seem easy in theory to combine the former with the higher
benefits of the latter there is yet but little doubt that such a union in
fact would never have been effected.

During this time it may well be supposed that my destination was
a frequent [subject?][11] of discourse between my parents. I was the
oldest and was of course to be the first to leave my father's roof. My
mother was strongly bent on having me placed in a counting house:
but as both her brothers were in Europe and as we had no other
friends who would be likely to interest themselves in bringing about
such an event and as it was out of the question to incur the expenses
with which my location with a stranger would be attended, she was
induced to acquiesce in my father's plan of giving me a trade. My
father's views on this subject were plausible enough in theory. In the
mere matter of being a mechanic there is nothing degrading. They
are one of the most useful branches of Society and they abound with
individual instances of the most estimable virtues. It is the most
reasonable and abstractly the most desirable thing in the world that
parents who are too poor to give their sons a learned profession or set
them up with a capital in business should put them to a trade and thus
furnish them with the means of an honest independence. But things
are stangely out of joint in this world and as Epictetus says every
thing here has two handles.[12] Thus to take the subject by the other
handle it is a most unreasonable—a most cruel thing—to take a boy
who has been brought up with some degree of moral delicacy and
place him among a set of semi-savages who are utter strangers to the

11. It appears that Seabury left a word out of is narrative. The text literally reads "a
frequent of discourse," but the context implies something akin to the above reading.

12. "Everything has two handles, by the one of which it ought to be carried and by
the other not," Epictetus (A.D. c. 50–c. 130), *Encheiridion*, 43. The significance of
Epictetus's observation is an important theme throughout the memoirs. See the
Introduction.

refinements of social life. The change in Physical comforts connected as they inseperably [*sic*] are with the finer feelings of our
nature is no small consideration. But the change in habits of sentiment and moral association is bitterly severe. You leave a state of
Society in which your feelings were respected for one in which they
are wontonly trifled with on every occasion; where retirement and
privacy are unknown: where to say nothing of piety or moral de-
portment every thing bordering on decorum or ordinary good
breeding is coarsely ridiculed; where you must be *vuglar* in the
lowest degree to escape the imputation of affecting to be *genteel*:
obscene and profane to escape being laughed at as a Quaker or a
Methodist: filthy and hoggish in the extreme to avoid being twitted
of vainness or pride.[13] A man that looks only at the manner in which
society ought to be framed may advocate his sons going to a trade:
but he that sees Society as it actually is may be allowed to shrink from
exposing his children to the pollution of vulgarity in its most dis-
gusting forms. I do not mean to say that young persons are exposed
to actual vice and crime any more in the workshop than they would
be in the counting house or at college. But they are brought in
contact with a different grade of it: they see the same degree of
turpitude clothed in a tenfold deformity. Whatever be the general
opinion I confess that for my own part when I came a few years after
this to read Paley's Moral Philosophy[14] there was no part of his
doctrine that I more heartily coincided in than that parents were
bound to give their children such a settlement in life as comported
with their own stations in society and the previous nurture of their
offspring.

The question of obligation however never presented itself in a
distinct shape to my father's mind. He wished to do the best he could
for his children and he had but little choice of opportunity. Of the

13. Quakers and Methodists were famous for their rigorous pietistic morality
which included a strict shunning of blasphemy and obscenity.
14. William Paley (1743–1805), *The Principles of Moral and Political Philosophy*, book
3, pt. 3, chap. 9, discusses parental responsibility in educating their children.

scenes to which he was about to introduce [me to?] he knew but little—my mother and myself still less. The prospect was held out to me in such a manner as to excite the last faculty which it would seem fitted to excite but the first which my mind was disposed to exercise—ambition. A trade—pursued with honesty, industry, and perseverence—which virtues I was exhorted to cherish—was represented as the sure though slow way to a respectable independence. The end was so palpable and pleasing that the means were naturally enough overlooked and I was quite willing to sail by a course which led to so desirable a harbour.[15]

In the fall of 1815 an incipient step was taken towards the accomplishment of a measure which now began to be eagerly anticipated by me and which was looked forward to—as I well remember—by my poor mother with mingled feelings of hope and dread. At the setting of the convention[16] my father made his annual visit to N[ew] York and succeeded in procuring for me the place which he desired. My services were wanted immediately and no time was to be lost in fitting me out. My mother set about the task with varied emotions and awaited the arrival of the day fixed for my departure as the most trying season of her life. I was the eldest and four brothers were to follow successively in my steps.[17] She regarded her separation from me as the first gash in the severance of her domestic ties. She felt it most bitterly: and as there is a natural connexion in calamities it recalled and renewed all the sorrows of her past life. She looked forward to it with melancholy presentiment. I was often with her in her own room. She would recount to me the story of her griefs with

15. In the manuscript Seabury had originally written "enter a road." The change in metaphor hints at an underlying motif in Seabury's work, the likening of human existence to the precarious existence of a ship at sea, where the will of the crew is constantly in battle with the blind forces of nature.

16. Seabury is referring to the annual convention of the Protestant Episcopal Church in the State of New York, that in 1815 met on 3–4 October at Trinity Church in New York City.

17. The other Seabury children were Charles Saltonstall, William, Edward, and Richard Francis. A daughter Mary Elizabeth had died in infancy.

the liveliest sensibility and would conjure up with her restless imagination the dangers that might await her children on that ocean of life to which she was about to commit them. She would one moment tremble with dread—another clasp me to her bosom and be dissolved in tears. Yet there was nothing extravagant in her grief. It was always controlled by a trust in Heavenly protection.

Three

At length the eventful day arrived when I was to leave the humble and happy home of my youth and commence my fortunes in the world. With what different emotions is such an occurence regarded by the child and the parent! For myself though entering on no very promising scene still my heart was beating with vague expectation! Little did I think that I should in future years revert to the associations I was then surrendering as the happiest of my life! Content and innoce[nt] I could not then forwise[1] for I had not experienced their opposites. One thing only weighed heavily on my heart and that was my mother's dejection. Her mind was covered with gloom. She clung to me as if we were about to part forever: and as I took my last embrace my heart sickened and some such vague presentiment seemed for a moment to paralyze my soul. But it soon passed over. It was a clear November morning and the cloudless sun and serene sky soon restored me to that cheerfulness of mind so congenial to a state of health as to be for any length of time inseparable from it. My father was in good spirits—the horse alone seemed at first to sympathise in the transient heaviness of my heart. Even after I recovered my vivacity the depression of the faithful beast seemed to continue— until finally he came to a dead halt and refused to carry me one step further from my father's house. I loved the beast and had taken good care of him for more than a year and I began to wonder whether there could be anything in that secret sympathy of which I had read existing in the brute creation. It was even so I had afterwards ample proof that it was the kind affection of his master's family that (at that

1. That is, foreknow. This is an example of the autodidact Seabury creating his own words. In the original manuscript he also has innocence for innocent.

58

painful hour of separation)[2] palsied the exertions of the faithful animal. For my next brother whose attachment to the horse was much more devoted than my own, thinking that his common fare was a poor preparation for so long a journey had on the night before our departure given him about a bushel of *Indian corn*! How many omens and secret sympathies of the Rosicrucian philosophy[3] might be explained by a groom or a hostler!

The day was short and the travelling bad so that we completed on that day only part of our journey. We spent the night at the house of a relative who had a son of about my age who was just prepared to enter college and expected to set off for Cambridge in the course of a few days.[4] I shall never forget the feelings with which on that evening I compared my destination with that of my cousin's. And I remember them not because they were particularly excited but because they were the first bleedings of that self pride which was afterwards so frequently and bitterly lacerated and was for some years the chief bane of my existence. My cousin was going to college an honor for which I felt I would have given the world—and I was going—even then I writhed at the thought—to learn a trade! But I shall have enough of such reflections as I proceed and I will not anticipate. We arrived at Brooklyn next morning between eleven and twelve o'clock and walked on board the ferry boat for N[ew] York. I had seen this large city twice before and was not therefore so much transported with surprise as to be unable to look around on our fellow passengers. At that moment one of the most important beings in the world in my estimation was the man under whose auspices my career was to commence—in other words, to whom I was Ɡoing [to be an] apprentice. Is it not possible I thought that he may be on board? There was a person that stood near me dressed in

2. The parenthetical phrase is found above the line in the manuscript.

3. The Rosicrucians were a religious group stemming from the perhaps legendary figure of Christian Rosenkreuz, which put great emphasis on esoteric wisdom and occult practices.

4. For Harvard College.

grey clothes—a middle aged man—with a considerable stoop in his shoulders and hard screwing features. I looked at him very attentively. He had two small eyes darting through the shaggy enclosures of a couple of pit holes that were sunk in his head—his lips were closely compressed and his nose and chin stood out somewhat in the attitude of a pair of open forceps. I could not help gazing at him and without thinking that this was naturally enough caused by the stare with which he was scrutinizing my father. I was again upon the point of building an air castle upon secret sympathy (in this case it could hardly be called attraction) when the gentleman approached my father with the question "A'n't you the gentleman that spoke to me some time ago about taking a boy?" "The very same," answered my father with his usual politeness, "and here is the young gentleman himself—my son Mr. Moneygripe!"[5] It was indeed the veracious Mr. Moneygripe! We interchanged a few words. He asked me how I should like my new employment? I told him in rather a studied phrase that I hoped to merit his approbation by my attention to my business. I thought he looked as if he did not expect much. But there was not much time for impressions favorable or otherwise: for as the boat reached the other side we parted.

About noon the next day my father parted from me and I proceeded with my trunk to Mr. Moneygripe's. His residence was a two story house with [a] brick front in the heart of the city. The front of the building both above and below was used as a warehouse. In the rear was a small addition which was used as a dwelling house and again in the rear of this was a large two story building which constituted the workshop. Under the workshop was a cellar which answered the double purpose of a kitchen and an eating room. Every part of the yard except a small alley that went round the building was piled with lumber; and a large frame in the extreme rear and a cellar

5. Another example of Seabury's playful use of pseudonyms. Circumstantial evidence seems to suggest that Mr. Moneygripe was in fact a Mr. William Mandeville, a furniture maker of some renown. At least according to Seabury's account, the name was appropriate, since money was a major concern to his employer.

under the warehouse were two other depositories for the same material. I did not at the time take much notice of the premises—though
I had ample opportunity afterwards to become acquainted with
them—being chiefly curious to obtain a view of my bedroom. The
probable nature of my accommodations had been a topic of conversation with my mother. She had formed in her mind a pretty distinct
idea of Mrs. Moneygripe—from what *data* I know not—certainly
not from a view of the original—and she thought it quite probable I
should have a room to myself and had given me very minute directions about keeping it in order. My fancy had accordingly pictured
my bed-room as a neat little apartment, with a handsome bedstead,
with a clean counterpin[6] turned down at the head so as to display the
linen sheets and white pillow cases to the best advantages—while
near by stood my wash-stand, wash-basin, soap and towel all for
once at least in good order for the reception of a newcomer. After
loitering about the yard for a few minutes I was told that I might
carry my trunk to my sleeping room and that John—whom for the
future I was to relieve of being the fag end of the shop—would show
me the way.[7] At the name of John I turned my eyes upon a dirty
vulgar looking fellow who approached and taking hold of one end of
the trunk and bidding me do the same by the other, very good
naturedly led the way to my lodging. Instead of entering the dwelling house, he made towards a pair of stairs that adjoined the workshop and I remember unconsciously expressing my surprise by asking him, "Are you sure this is the way?" at which he naturally
enough laughed and replied he had seen it often enough to know it.
We ascended two flights of steps and at the end of the second which
was dark and winding he pushed open a small shutter and shoving
my trunk into one corner announced in a style of his own that my
apartment was before me. I beheld the scene with an amazement
which I was yet afraid to express. It was a small garret room under a

6. That is, a counterpane or bedspread.
7. The fag end was the last part or coarse end of a piece of cloth and hence
figuratively was the worst part of a job, usually assigned to the youngest apprentice.

sloping shingled roof the highest part of it barely admitting of a man's standing upright. It had but one light and that was a window consisting of four small panes of glass. On the floor—which certainly had never been washed—lay two large beds—covered each with a filthy looking blanket and a black spread. Sheets fortunately there were none: for two or three dirty looking pillow cases afforded as much of such material as one would ever wish to behold. Really for the moment I sickened at the sight—and yet as I said—I was afraid to show my feelings. I ventured however to ask in a faltering tone, "*Do they all sleep here?*" "O yes—all six of us—good times we have of it too." "May be," I said "there is another room?" without daring to express the faint hope which I still felt of having a separate apartment. "O no—you'll sleep over there," pointing to the corner bed " 'tween Alf and me—always put the last comer in the middle." "But where do you wash?" "Wash? Wash out doors—when the weather ain't too cold—and when it is we don't wash at all—do just as you're a mind to—except Sunday mornings then we always take a good scrub." I found that there was no alternative and so prepared to submit to my fate with as good a grace as I could. We then came down stairs and went into the workshop—where my companion—who naturally looked on me as an important acquisition on whom he was henceforward to turn off the most disagreeable part of his labors—spent a few minutes in giving me an insight into the character of my fellow apprentices. The oldest was John Sobersides—the son of a respectable farmer at Jamaica[8]—very steady—best apprentice Baas had ever had[9]—would be out of his time in about six months. The next was Ike Redface—a rale clever fellow[10]—a better

8. Jamaica, New York, a town in Queens county, about twelve miles from Manhattan.

9. Baas is a Dutch word, meaning employer or boss, that was only beginning to creep into common usage at this time. See W. J. Rorabaugh, *The Craft Apprentice: From Franklin to the Machine Age in America* (New York: Oxford University Press, 1986), 135.

10. An attempt by Seabury to capture dialect.

hand at work than the other, but he liked a horn of brandy and would lie as fast as a horse could trot. The next was Bill SaintJohn—hadn't been here long—thought himself a pretty smart chap—was always reading when he got a chance and could talk *dic* (dictionary words) equal to any fellow. The fourth was Alf Hothead—a good natured fellow—if you'd let him have his way—but a most a hell of a temper[*sic*]—throw a jack-plane at your head as quick as [a] wink. After being duly stared at and catechized by these *ourang outangs*[11] I was fain to retreat from the mahogany dust which was the breathing material of the shop and betake myself for variety to the Warehouse. Here I encountered the awful Mr. Moneygripe—who compassion- ating[12] my vacuity of mind pointed to a large pile of maple joist[s] that lay in the street and ordered me to carry them into the yard and pile them up. I sprung with great alacrity—determined to prepossess him in my favor by the activity of my movement and commenced shouldering the joist[s] and carrying them one by one to the ap- pointed place. They were prodigiously heavy and I soon worked myself tired. I perservered however till tea time: when I was sum- moned with the five mahogany faces to surround which our betters had just left. If I wanted anything to complete the surprise inspired by the lodging room I had it in full when a squalid looking servant woman who had been wasting over the fire seated herself at the table to perform the equally arduous tasks of *pouring out* tea for others and *pouring* it *into* herself.[13] I remember nothing at this distance of the rest of the evening except [the] horror I felt of being compelled to sleep between two persons whom I could not bear to have near me and under coverings which I was afraid to touch. As bedtime approached however I found myself exceedingly sleepy and my bones aching from the weight of the joist[s]. My squeamishness at length yielded

11. The contemporary spelling of orangutan. Here again Seabury was trying to emphazise the perceived social barrier between himself and the other members of the workshop.

12. That is, having compassion for.

13. That is, eating along with the servants the leftovers from the master's table.

to necessity—I threw myself down trying to shrink into as small a compass as I could—I very soon forgot my troubles and partook of the refreshment of *kind nature's sweet restorer*[14]—which sheds as balmy an influence on the filthy straw of a garret as on the soft down of a palace.

14. Seabury here is quoting from Edward Young's *Night Thoughts*, book one, line one. The citation is from memory since the line actually reads, "Tired nature's sweet restorer, balmy sleep."

Four

It can hardly be supposed that so important a night would pass without dreams. Of these I remember but one. My mother had stood by me urging me with the most affectionate persuasions to read my bible and make its precepts the guide of my conduct—adding that in answer to her prayers I was now about to be favored with a supernatural testimony to its truth. She then left me and immediately there appeared before me an old grey bearded man with a staff in one hand and a bible in the other. "Child," he said, "you once laughed at the story of Balaam's ass—but look there!"[1] My guilty conscience threw me into a panic but turning my eyes in the direction in which he pointed I beheld one of the long eared tribe and a man with a drawn sword mounted on his back. "Listen," he said—and as he spoke the animal opened his mouth and uttered one of the strangest volumes of sound that had ever assailed my ears. I started involuntarily. The beast again poured forth a braying noise that was evidently broken into words though I could not distinguish what they were. I sat upright in bed, rubbed my eyes, looked about the room and saw several persons running about in great confusion. The same roaring was instantly repeated which I now understood to be nothing less (more it could not be) than the stentorian voice of Mr. Moneygripe summoning his boys to work. I lost no time in dressing myself though I found with all the dispatch I could use that the room was cleared before I had got half my clothes on. I made the best of my way down and while looking around for a basin of water (for I never

1. The story of the prophet Balaam and his ass is recounted in the Bible in Numbers 22. In the story the ass is given the gift of speech to warn Balaam of God's judgment, and the story has traditionally been used to show that God could use any instrument for communication.

felt more the need of ablution) was ordered to the warehouse. Here I found that what was to be hence forward my first morning act—the opening of the door and windows—was already performed. I was now set to rubbing up the furniture and was given to understand that by this process I was every morning to gain my appetite for breakfast. After breakfast I went into the workshop and was ordered to make a pot of glue and by way of great favor was shown how to do it after being first called a nincompoop for my ignorance. Very soon I was told to shoulder a couple of mahogany joist[s] and carry them to the turners in ——— St.,[2] and bring back a couple more which I should there find worked into the shape of bedposts. On my return I saw on the steps a hand barrow with a couple of straps and had the pleasure of helping one of my seniors place on this a sideboard and carry it to the house of its purchaser. In the afternoon something similar was to be done and every day brought with it a similar round of business.

All this corresponded so little with my expectations that I could not help expressing my surprise to my companion. In answer to several questions that I put him he told me that those who got such a place as we had were pretty well off—they had good fare and though old Moneygripe was as cross as the Devil yet he took it all out in jaw—and never beat or abused them—and as to running of errands and such sort of things the youngest apprentice had to do it for a year before he tried his hand at the tools. This information galled me considerably—I determined however to bear my year's indignity as patiently as I could consoling myself with the hope that after it was passed I should have easier times and a more creditable station.

Many of the incidents of the following winter are still fresh in my recollection and the occasional obtrusions on my thoughts brings over my face one of those infernal scowls that, as my friends tell me,

2. Turners or lathe workers were scattered throughout lower Manhattan. The New York City directory of 1816 locates them (among other places) on Orange, William, Beekman, and Nassau streets, any of which could have been the one referred to by Seabury.

every now and then deform my face. It can answer no good purpose to mention them. *Haec olim meminisse juvabit*[3] will apply to a small portion of my story and to this as little as any. The degradation to which I was continually subjected was horrible. The most galling was carrying furniture about the streets on hand barrows, assisting to place it in a gentleman's parlor or to put up a bedstead in a lady's chamber. Another thing that especially gnawed my feelings was the taking of the money that gentlemen are in the habit of bestowing on menials for services of this sort. At first I made some demur to this habit—but was soon laughed out of my feelings or rather into a suppression of them; finding that occasional mortifications of pride were more easily endured than the incessant gibes of ridicule. Improvement of any kind was out of the question. I borrowed two or three volumes of the Tatler and Spectator[4] and at the expense of becoming an object of derision used to read them sometimes when I could get the benefit of a light and a seat by the kitchen fire. The employment of the days however was fatiguing and by nine o'clock I was generally glad enough to crawl into my lair.

I cannot help thinking that it is a wise arrangement in the moral economy of God to render the worst affections of our nature subservient frequently to the best ends. In theory every allotment of life may be borne with a reasonable degree of contentment and sufficient incentives will be found in strictly Christian motives to better our outward circumstances and to turn the circumstances themselves to the improvement of our minds. But in fact the case, even with good men, has been otherwise. It is discontent with one condition of life that leads us to aspire to another: and when we have once embarked on our course it is pride, ambition or vanity that fills our sails and

3. *Aeneid* 1.203. Roughly translated the passage reads "may this distress some day be a joy to recall."

4. The *Tatler* was a periodical (1709–11) edited by Richard Steele under the pseudonym Issac Bickerstaff. It was succeeded by the *Spectator*, whose most important essays were composed by Joseph Addison. Both were often reprinted and became a model of English prose style.

speeds us on our way. How far these instincts of our unrenewed nature are legitimate springs of conduct is a nice question of casuistry which the person who is under the influence is ill fitted and less disposed to solve or examine. Very probably at the time when he is chiefly called on for action he has not thought of analyzing his motives: or if he is conscious of any unchristian passion reigning in his bosom there is something in the pungency of his case that leads him to justify it. This was exactly my own situation. My pride was continually bleeding and I felt that it was impossible to bear its reiterated wounds.

There was one feature in my circumstances that tended to aggravate my situation and nurture the tormenting feeling of which I have spoken. My associates on evenings or on Sundays when I made visits were of a very different class in Society from the tenants of the workshop. Had it been otherwise I might have quietly sunk down to the level of the shop or the garret. My aunt by my father's side who for the most part took practical and common sense views of life and heartily approved of the choice which my father had made for me took great pride in having me known to all the acquaintances of our family.[5] Here perhaps I would meet persons on a footing of equality in the evening who would pass me in the streets next morning with a handbarrow or a bed post in a dress not fit for a *sans-culotte*.[6] An aunt by my mother's side was married to a physician of eminence and moved in the first circles of the city.[7] It was seldom that I could be induced to visit her family: and when I did I always returned with feelings of the deepest chagrin. Probably I was well treated and certainly I was always spoken to with affection. But I was constantly apprehending slights and therefore it was natural enough sometimes

5. This is probably a reference to either Abigail Mumford or Mary Seabury in whose school Seabury was later to assist. See letter eight, note 6.

6. Literally, without breeches. It was the term used to describe the extreme republican party of the French Revolution which rejected the short clothes of the aristocracy.

7. This probably refers to Abigail Saltonstall who was married to Dr. William Handy, a physician then residing in the city.

to imagine that I had received them. The conversation too frequently turned on persons to whose houses I occasionally attended on menial offices and once or twice I was seated by a lady in the evening to whose parlor I had carried a dozen chairs in the morning. And as if the silent endurance of my own feelings was not enough my aunt Affable (who considered herself a customer of Mr. Moneygripe and took no small credit to herself for her agency in procuring me the enviable situation) was sure to catechize me about the particulars of my business and leave no question unasked which might help her company to understand that I was a poor connexion at a trade whom she in the midst of her splendor was not ashamed to disown. For a person to bear all of this that had sense enough to see and to feel it was impossible. To one of my temperament it was agony. Often have I left her house cursing my miserable lot: and I remember one evening in particular, after some occurrence of this kind, as I was walking down Broadway breaking out into an audible soliloquy—the tears coursing down my cheeks and my voice broken with sobs—"It is Pride—is it? And what if it is pride? Doesn't pride cause as much suffering as any feeling? And doesn't it as much deserve to be respected?"

Such were the feelings and incidents that by rendering me discontented with my lot ultimately contributed to my emancipation from it. This event however was still distant and before it happened I was compelled to endure the heaviest affliction that has ever befallen me.

But before I mention this I will refer to a few circumstances connected with my religious experience. I had left my father's house with an equally strong attachment to the church and aversion to every thing not belonging to it that bore the name of religion.[8] My residence in the house of a Presbyterian and in a place that abounded [with] dissenters and sectaries of every description as did the city of Gotham was lamented as an evil against the danger of which I was

8. Seabury, following the traditional English pattern, referred to the Episcopal Church simply as the church and non-Episcopalians simply as dissenters.

duly cautioned. A prayerbook was given me as the best amulet to preserve me from every species of demoniacal possession and I was strictly charged and affectionately exhorted to attend the church regularly and the church alone; a charge which I had no temptation to break as any deviation from it could not have been more repugnant to any person's feelings than my own. I found no difficulty in a regular attendance on church, but considerable difficulty in regulating my conduct at home. Few men indeed were more fervently pious than Mr. Moneygripe. He had prayers in his family every night and was frequently overheard praying in the course of the day. But his religion never reached as far as his workshop: though never did a set of Heathens need conversion more than its inmates. He governed by severity and as was natural every advantage was taken of his absence; while obscene songs and profane language were the coin chiefly current. Of course there were frequent conflicts in my mind between my principles and practice and they ended as is too commonly the case in degrading the former to support the latter instead of raising the latter [to] dignify and strengthen the former. When however religion itself or any of its doctrines was openly attacked I defended it as far as opportunity allowed. Among the journeymen upstairs was a Deist of the Tom Paine school; of smooth face, sharp nose, sharp chin and a pair of little black twinkling eyes. He was crabbed and seldom spoke: but sometimes when excited by an extra glass of brandy and water he would become the oracle of the shop.[9] His chief themes were the doctrines of the atonement and incarnation which he ridiculed in a style the coarsest and most horrible that I had ever heard.[10] In endeavoring to recollect my impressions of this person I cannot find that this rant struck into my mind a

9. Another play on words. The term *oracle* was often used in Deist literature both in England (such as by Charles Blount, *The Oracles of Reason* [1693]) and in America perhaps most famously by Ethan Allen in *Reason the Only Oracle of Man* . . . (1784).

10. Both the doctrines of the atonement, or the understanding of the saving work of Jesus Christ, and the incarnation, or the belief that God became human in the person of Jesus, were favorite points of attack by Deists.

spark of skepticism. He advanced no argument and he was too passionate to listen to any. It had an effect however more deeply and permanently injurious. It filled my mind with images and associations that marred the simplicity and purity of devotion: images and associations which unfortunately have been been since too frequently renewed to permit of their ever being wholly effaced. Below stairs among the apprentices—religion was never except casually a topic of remark until about the middle of the winter Alf Hothead was converted and turned suddenly from singing songs and swearing to quoting scripture and repeating aloud all prayers and collects in the prayerbook. I was but a child and was incapable of estimating the defects of his character and was naturally drawn nearer to him from his devotion and his preference for the church. I accompanied him several times to a prayer meeting and can remember deriving a serious gratification from the piety that was manifested and the more so when after repeated doubts and enquiries I was fully convinced that the majority of the meeting were Episcopalians: being satisfied that a few Methodists or Presbyterians could do no material injury. I soon found however that Alf's religion was mere whitewash. His temper was the same: though to be sure it was displayed in a holier cause; while the fervor of his devotion (probably without his attending it) served as a lullaby to his conscience to encourage him in the grossest sensuality. To the credit of his prayer meeting however I ought to add that he soon exchanged it for one of a more liberal character. He became a hot Universalist and regularly twice a week equipped himself in weapons fresh from the armory of a Mr F[oster][11] one as I should then have termed him of the schismatics of

---

11. The Universalist preacher was quite possibly John Foster, who had a congregation for a time at first on Rose Street and later on Broadway, near Pearl Street. The length of his ministry (which began around 1803) is unclear, but contemporary accounts note that he was known both for his eloquence and the controversy which his ministry provoked. See Richard Eddy, *Universalism in America: A History*, 2 vols., 3d ed. (Boston: Universalist Publishing House, 1894), 1:536–37; and John W. Francis, *Old New-York: or Reminiscences of the Past Sixty Years* (New York, 1858), 136–37.

The Letters

modern time. I was now frequently pitted against the apostate churchman in argument and though in most instances I was apparently triumphant yet there were several of his arguments to which I secretly attached more importance than I was willing to allow—and was more than once surprised to find him backing out just at the time when I thought I was vanquished. Several texts I then reserved for examination at a future time: nor did I forget them when I had afterwards access to my father's books.[12]

I was thus situated in mind and body when an approaching confirmation was notified from St. Paul's pulpit[13] and my friends admonished me to become a candidate. Confirmation I knew to be an excellent thing and an ordinance of the church.[14] I had frequently heard my mother speak in strains of warmest praise of several exemplary young persons who, at a suitable age had come forward, affirmed their baptismal vows and had been confirmed by the bishop. My father too had frequently told me that Confirmation was a rite of Apostolic origin, that it consisted in the ratification of baptismal vows and that when I was old enough it would be proper for me to comply with it. It was natural that I should feel ambitious to emulate

12. The basic doctrine of the Universalists was their belief in the universal salvation of all persons. One of their standard criticisms of the traditional Christian position was the difficulty of reconciling the traditional faith in a God of love with the further belief that that God condemned all who had never heard the Christian message to damnation. It was precisely this question that Seabury was to tackle in his most provocative theological essay "The Salvability of the Heathen" (published in 1838) which attempted to find a middle ground between the traditional Christian position and Universalism.

13. St. Paul's Chapel was one of the two chapels of Trinity Church. Both Trinity Church and the chapels (the other being St. John's) were served by the clergy of Trinity parish which at this time were Bishop John Henry Hobart, William Berrian, Thomas Yardley How, and Benjamin T. Onderdonk.

14. Since until the close of the American revolution the American Episcopal Church had possessed no bishops, the only American Episcopalians who could receive the episcopal ordinance of confirmation were those few who could travel to England. Most colonial Episcopalians accordingly put little emphasis upon the rite. It was hence the concern of Episcopal writers during the early nineteenth century to emphasize anew the importance of this practice.

those whom I had heard commended and conform to the usages of the church to which every thing in the shape of opposition was sure to excite the *espirit de corps*. Accordingly I expressed my willingness to be confirmed. Etiquette required that I should announce the attention [intention?] to a clergyman and one of my aunts very kindly offered to accomany me to Dr. Rubric's.[15] I found the Dr. in the midst of his family comfortably seated in a rocking chair by the parlour fire. After some preliminary questions about my father, etc., he opened the subject by saying, "You understand, I presume, the nature of Confirmation?" "O yes sir." "It is," he quickly resumed, "the assumption of our baptismal obligations and a public profession of our willingness to conform to the precepts of Christ's religion and a rite too, in which . . ." I sat upon nettles being mightily piqued that he should consider me ignorant of so important an ordinance of the church. "Yes," I said, "it was the ratification of the vows our sponsors made for us in baptism and a rite in which we received further grace from God to assist us in the discharge of our duty."[16] "Yes, yes," he added, "I have no doubt you have been well grounded in all these matters—your father and your grandfather were great friends of the church and I hope you will always follow in their paths"; and then giving me a couple of pamphlets of Bishop H[obart] on the subject he changed the conversation.[17] The question whether I was spiritually qualified for the ordinance was one which it did not occur to Dr. R. to suggest and in the affirmative of which I tactily acquiesced without even, to the best of my remembrance,

15. Dr. Rubric was probably Thomas Yardley How, both because he was the only "doctor" among the assistants (he had received a D.D. from Columbia College in 1812) and also because contemporary accounts of his character seem to confirm Seabury's observations. See in particular *The Letters of John Pintard*, 4 vols. (New York, 1940–41), 1:113.

16. Both Rubric and Seabury are quoting to each other formal, schoolboy definitions of the rite of confirmation. In light of his long family heritage, Seabury evidently was affronted by Rubric's condescension toward him.

17. John Henry Hobart's pamphlet, *The Candidate for Confirmation Instructed . . .* was first published in 1816 under the title *A Sermon Explaining the Order of Confirmation*.

formally proposing it to my mind.[18] The preparation however on which I entered was of great benefit to me. The sermon I read—yet without obtaining much new information: and though the place was necessarily extremely unfavorable to spiritual ablutions in which bodily ones were but seldom performed yet I availed myself of such occasions as occurred to offer the prescribed prayers and I hope I shall not be deemed uncharitable if I express my doubts whether the old garret has ever before or since witnessed a similar act of devotion. On the whole I have no doubt that the rite would have proved to me a means of grace and confirmation if I had then been permitted to receive it—but from this I was prevented by an event to which I have already alluded and the more particular mention of which I reserve for the next chapter.

18. The question Seabury alludes to would be a long standing issue in his church's theology. In order to distinguish Episcopal piety from the surrounding evangelicalism with its emphasis upon a subjective conversion experience, individuals such as How and Hobart chose rather to emphasize the objective nature of Episcopal sacramentalism. Yet their critics claimed they did so by sacrificing the necessity of moral commitment. As a theological writer Seabury would later attempt to bring these two concerns together in an overarching view of the sacraments.

Five

It was on a raw unpleasant afternoon in the month of March when I had been sent to procure a set of castors at the Hardware Store and on my return found Mr. Moneygripe with a couple of his boys in the warehouse impatiently waiting for me. I thought I observed something grave and inquisitive in the countenance of the boys—a look that I can hardly describe but which excited a transient feeling of alarm. Moneygripe however gave me a gruff reception and after grumbling in a tone of voice between a bray and a growl at the length of my absence told me that my uncle had called for me and that I must go immediately to his house. I went out biting my lips with vexation: and so strong was this feeling at the moment that had not the countenance of the boys excited ominous apprehensions I should have felt no curiosity as to the object of my uncle's call. Afterwards when I could revert to the melancholy intelligence which I received and of which Moneygripe was at the time possessed there was nothing in all his conduct that ever stung me more than the entire destitution or rather the positive barbarity of feeling which he then evinced. I will briefly mention the event which my aunt so affectionately and circuitously opened to me. My father had written in unutterable anguish that my mother was dead and that the funeral was waiting in order that I might follow her to the grave. It was but a fortnight before that I had received from her one of those affectionate letters which I still cherish as the sacred and almost the only relics of maternal love. Of my feelings I will will say nothing. I had but little time however to indulge them. I was obliged to return to Mr. M[oneygripe]'s for my clothes. I waited till it was dark that I might enter unobserved. In returning from my garret I was obliged to pass with a light the room in which Moneygripe was sitting. He could not help seeing me and after I was in the entry came out and said in a whining tone that as I was going home perhaps I should want some money and offered me a dollar. I had not courage at that moment to refuse— but the reception of that dollar from a wretch who not an hour before had insulted my feelings under circumstances in which a savage would have respected them will ever be among the memorabilia of my life! Next morning I set off on my melancholy journey and reached home on the day following. My father caught me in his arms and clasped me to his bosom. It was an unusual mode for him to testify his affection and therefore I remember it. A short time after he led me down stairs to the door of the front room, which he opened, silently motioned for me to enter and left me. I beheld a coffin and found myself alone with my mother's corpse: in the very room too in which but a few months before I had watched her tearful eye and had been softened by her affectionate counsels! I approached the coffin and looked on her features. The *passion* of grief subsided with a gush of tears; and then there succeeded a few moments in which for once Heaven reigned in my bosom!

I pass over the melancholy incidents of this day and the following. One trifling circumstance I will mention because it has often occurred [to] me as being one of the first developments of an unhappy trait of character. As we were leaving the spot that has ever since been consecrated as the depository of all that in my early recollections was most pure and lovely, the minister of the Presbyterian congregation approached and accosted me in the language of condolence at my recent loss. In an instant the sentiment of grief was exchanged for anger and offended pride. I said nothing—thanks be to the sainted being, of whom I was just bereaved, whose early lessons of self government have enabled on this and many similar occasions to suppress the rebellious passions of my heart. Another circumstance too so illustrates my father's character and thus indirectly the principles in which I was educated that I cannot prevail on myself to withhold it. After my mother's demise one of the first steps which my father had taken was to send for Mr. H[art] of Hempstead, the nearest Episcopal clergyman—who resided at a distance of more than thirty miles.[1] On the day of the funeral he was informed that Mr. H[art] could not come but that Mr. G[reen],[2] the Presbyterian clergyman of the place had expressed a willingness to perform any services that might be required. This he promptly declined and avowed his determination of reading the burial service himself and dispensing with all other services—a thing very unusual in the country.[3] This he did in a firm manly voice though evidently struggling with the deepest emotion. And it would have melted any man's heart to have seen the husband at the tomb of his wife thus suffering as a martyr to the feelings of the Christian. Could I help loving a religion for which I was taught, by such impressive lessons, to cherish an exclusive regard?

Every emotion of the mind consists of two elements—sentiment and passion. The distinction is obvious: sentiment is eternal, passion, particularly in youth, is evanescent. Thus it happens that though I have ever cherished the tenderest recollection of my mother a few days restored me, in spite of myself, to an occasional buoyancy of spirits. I looked forward however with dread to the day of my return; and felt as if I would give the world to escape from the fangs of Moneygripe and the contamination of his workshop. I deter-

1. Seth Hart was rector of St. George's Church Hempstead, Long Island. Ironically, he had also been ordained to the priesthood in 1792 by Seabury's grandfather, Bishop Seabury.

2. A reference possibly to the Rev. Zechariah Green, who was at the time the Presbyterian minister at Setauket. See E. H. Gillett, *The History of the Presbyterian Church in the United States of America*, 2 vols. (Philadelphia, 1864), 2:96.

3. Two factors probably contributed to this seemingly ill-tempered reaction. The first was a sense of personal snub. Since Hart was a far more distinguished clergyman with connections to the Seabury family, his failure to respond at this time of personal loss was considered an affront. Second, as rigorous high church Episcopalians, neither the elder nor the younger Seabury accepted Presbyterians as true ministers of Christ's church since they did not receive valid (that is, Episcopal) ordinations. The idea of a "dissenter" leading the funeral service would have been theologically abhorent.

mined frequently to make a strong appeal to my father—but whenever I attempted it *vox faucibus haesit*[4]—feeling choked my utterance and I was fain to defer the painful topic which my father I saw was far from courting. At length came the evening of the day which was appointed for my departure. I packed up my trunk with a heavy heart and, after prayers when the family had dispersed, lingered around my father determined to unburden my griefs. The agitation of that night I shall never forget. It was sometime before I could get the use of my voice but when I did I told him all I had to say—the mortifications of pride, the taunts of ridicule, the temptations which I encountered and the pollutions to which I was exposed. He heard me and soothed me with the most affectionate sympathy. "But my son," he said, "how can it be helped? I am poor—could I afford to give you an education nothing would be more truly grateful to my heart—but this you well know is out of the question—and there is no other way for you than to bear these crosses with patience and to trust that the good providence of God has better times in reserve for you." My father was a man of little energy of character but of the tenderest feelings. I saw that he was affected—and my own griefs were for the time merged in the regret that I had awakened his. What he had said too was reasonable: and I was obliged to acquiesce.

My mother died on the 22d. of March 1816 and by the middle of the next month my nose was again filled with the effluvia of glue and mahogany dust. I found Moneygripe in a high state of exacerbation which rendered him like all kindred animals, extremely dangerous of approach. The reason was, as I soon ascertained, that Alf Hothead had fixed his affections on Patty the servant maid and vowed with the ardour of a true lover that he would marry her—and thus Moneygripe was in a feverish dread of either losing four years of his apprentice's time or being taxed with certain pledges of affection which he could not anticipate with any better grace from never having been blessed with any children of his own. The consequence

---

4. "The words clung to my mouth."

of this romantic attachment I may not disclose and must therefore treat it as Moneygripe did the heroine of the story with a dismissal. In other respects things were going on as usual. It was but a few evenings after my return that my agency was required—as it had been several times before—in purchasing the materials of a treat—an assortment, that is, of crackers, cheese and brandy levied in right of the immemorial prescription by the inmates of a workshop, on every new coming journeyman. This was a practice of the most demoralizing kind. One at least was found who could sing a smutty song: business was suspended and the evening passed away in a rapid circulation of Infidel ribaldry and obscene mirth. I mention this now that I think of it in order to adduce a statement which I have lately observed in a report of the N[ew] Y[ork] Temperance Society that this mischievous custom is, in consequence of the efforts of the Society, to a great extent abolished.[5]

Fresh occurrences were happening every day to disgust me with my situation until at length the feeling of discontent caused an habitual dejection of spirits that combined with the labor which I was compelled to undergo, to injure my health. The subject of my indentures[6] was now alluded to—and as this had always been offensive so it was now particularly alarming. I had resolved never to be bound. The event however was now in prospect and I saw that something must speedily be done. In this state of doubt and perplexity an accident happened which decided my fate.

I ought to [sic] first to mention that I had been lately occasionally promoted to the use of the saw and the jackplane. This however was far from reconciling me to my lot. The truth is I had a most astonishing inaptitude for all mechanical employments which those who

5. *First Annual Report of the New York State Temperance Society* (New York, 1830). Pages 19 through 29 of the *Report* deal with temperance among mechanics and pages 22–24 deal particularly with the decline of public "treats" or the custom of purchasing liquor by an apprentice who had come of age, that is, become a journeyman.

6. An indenture legally bound an apprentice to a master for a set number of years as well as enumerating the master's responsibilities. The text suggests that up to this point Seabury was involved in a trial period.

dealt in plain English (and some others alas! were near me) used to denominate stupidity. In truth though I could sit down and take in the drift of a book with as much pleasure and profit as most boys yet I was always most wo[e]fully destitute of what the Yankees significantly call *gumption*. If my garrulity may be pardoned I will mention an instance of this which occurred a year or two before the time of which I am now writing. I had taken passage in a small wood sloop for N[ew] Y[ork] and was extremely anxious to distinguish myself by such services as I could render. Not content with tugging at the oar when the vessel was becalmed or working at the gib when she tacked, I aspired when occasion offerred, to holding the helm. We had proceeded as far as Throg's Neck[7] when the wind having nearly died away the captain called to me and begged to steer the vessel in the direction which he mentioned. I took the helm and fixed my eye on the compass with some little feeling of importance when he retired to the cabin leaving me sole master of the deck. It was about ten o'clock at night—I kept my post for more than two hours when I began to grow excessively sleepy—and perceiving that there was little or no wind thought I might venture to lash the helm fast to the railings of the quarter deck and take a berth with the rest. I did so, not however without some apprehension for the result. And indeed I had reason for the apprehension—for it is impossible to describe the torture with which on the next day I received the gibes from all hands on my skill in steering a vessel at anchor. If I were to attempt to explain this phenomenon on philosophical grounds in order to defend myself from the charge of stupidity I suppose I should only the more convince my readers that I deserved it. I will therefore only say that this faculty or rather want of faculty was continually bringing me into difficulty. I could not even saw a board without making the instrument move in every direction but the right one. The incident so important in turning the sealer of my destiny was of the same

7. A finger of land in the southeastern part of the Bronx jutting into the Long Island Sound.

kind. Some furniture was purchased for transportation and I was ordered to make a packing box. The dimensions were given me and I set about the task. After it was completed I found that the article to be packed was of the same dimensions with the *outside* of the box instead of the *inside*! I flung the hammer upon the ground, went up stairs and packed my trunk and in the course of half an hour took an eternal adieu of Moneygripe and all his concerns. Thus it happened as with many revolutions of greater moment that an accident accomplished in an instant what reason had been long endeavoring, in vain, to achieve.

Before my readers take a final farewell of Moneygripe I must beg them not to do him injustice. He was, or rather is, as the world goes an honest man, a good citizen and above all a deacon in the church. He has now become an assistant alderman of the city and his name frequently appears in the reports of the Common Council.[8] No doubt there are many such men who have apprentices; and it would be well if the friends of moral reform would use their influence with men of this description, by means of public measures, to meliorate this condition of Society. Such men might be induced from a sense of character to extend to their apprentices and others some of the benefits of Christian discipline. They might at least be brought to include them in their family devotions: avarice might grudge the time but pride would make the sacrifice.

8. Mandeville was assistant alderman of the third ward of New York City in 1830 and 1831. In 1832 he became alderman for the same ward.

Six

This bend in the current of my life took place, I think, in the month of June when I had just completed my fifteenth year. It was on Friday evening that I went on board the sloop and we did not reach the end of our sail until Sunday morning and then we were obliged to come to anchor at the harbor's mouth—a distance of about four miles from my father's. I accepted an invitation from Mr. ——— a young lawyer and great man of the place to accompany him to his father's which was nearby, who attended church at S——— and in whose wagon I could get a conveyance home.[1]

My arrival excited considerable surprise which did not however diminish the cordiality of my reception. I went to church with my father and had thus ample time to set my thoughts in order before I explained to him the reasons of my sudden appearance. This I did with tolerable candour except that I suppressed the story of the packing box. He regretted very much that I could not have been contented with my situation but trusted as usual that Providence would overrule all things for the best. I could very fairly too make some pretensions to ill health—a plea that never fails to gain upon a parent's heart. This together with the pleasure of seeing one another reconciled me to my home and my friends to my company for at least two or three months. But towards the end of this time the questions frequently occurred to my mind—and never without exciting a painful interest: "*What shall I do? What can I do? What am I fit for?*" From no quarter could I discern a ray of light. In one thing only

---

1. All of the above paragraph, save the first sentence, was crossed out, presumably by Seabury, at some point after it was written. About twenty-one more lines have been doubly crossed out and are largely illegible. These lines seem to recount a somewhat flirtatious breakfast with the lawyer's sisters.

was I fixed—not to return to a trade and I believe I would at that moment sooner have died than have set foot in a workshop or inhaled another respiration of mahogany dust. But nowhere else had I a prospect of a livelihood. The thought of a mercantile life was little more desirable and the attainment of a profession seemed as impracticable as a ride to the summit of Mount Blanc or Chimborazo.[2] One thing only seemed to afford a gleam of hope. There were men I knew that got their living by surveying. I was pretty confident I could master this art and thought I should like the practice of it. I pondered over this project for about an hour—at the end of which time I had surveyed a number of farms and my services were in great demand by all the land holders in the county. To be sure this was imagination. But didn't I know something of surveying? And couldn't I learn it thoroughly? And this done what was to prevent my having plenty of business? I asked my father if there were any man in this part of the country that followed this profession—for with this epithet I did not hesitate to dignify my destined employment.[3] He told me that there was an elderly gentleman—a Mr. Saxon—who lived about [?] miles distant that was in high repute. "An *elderly* gentleman, sir, did you say?" "Yes, and poor man he is at present in very bad health." My heart beat quick—I shall certainly succeed him, I thought to myself—"Has he much business, sir?" "Very little my son." Which thought I, how can it be otherwise? Old and sick besides—but all the better chance for me. Full of this project I ran up stairs, furnished myself with Flint's Surveying, a sheet of pasteboard and an old case of instruments and in a very short time projected a traverse table and a diagram and had my head full of logarithms, sines, tangents, and cosines. Within a week I had read half through the book and obtained the dimensions of all the rectangular

2. Mount Blanc is the highest mountain peak in the Alps; Chimborazo is the highest in Ecuador, and during Seabury's lifetime it was believed to be the highest mountain in the Andes.

3. Surveying was technically not a profession, but in Seabury's mind it had become so.

pieces of ground in the neighborhood. There was only one difficulty—I had no instruments with which to take bearing and angles
and should not know how to use them if I had them. Of course my
project was carefully disguised from every person and my father
particularly was the last person to whom I would entrust it while
thus in embryo but the first, I thought, to whom I would communi-
cate it when my present obstacles were surmounted. I was therefore
obliged to be cautious. "Is Mr. Saxon, sir," I asked, "an Episcopa-
lian?" "Why, my son, I have been told by the old people of the
congregation that he formerly *was* a churchman—but he lives at a
great distance and I believe has married into a dissenting family
and—in fact, seldom or ever comes to church." "But, father, I
wonder you don't visit him? "To tell the truth I have often thought
of doing so but have always been prevented by some untoward
incident or other." "Why can't you take it in your way, sir, when
you go to Islip?"[4] "Haven't time my son, it is a mile off the road."
"But why not spend Saturday night there and drive over to church in
the morning?" "Well really, I never once thought of that but now
you mention it, I think the plan is a good one." This was precisely
the point I wished to bring about as I had no doubt of procuring the
favour of Mr. S[axon] to teach me the instruments and perhaps give
me an invitation or, if not, accept of an offer which I was determined
to make him, if necessary, to accompany him in his next surveying
expedition. My father's next visit to Islip was between two and three
weeks off—and the time, as I counted it hour by hour, seemed to
be interminable. Before it arrived however my anticipations were
blasted. For riding, one day in the interim, with my father, we
passed through a piece of meadow land where we observed two or
three men walking barefoot over the marsh and exposed to the
blazing rays of a noon day sun. One of them—an old man with a pair
of ragged trousers, an old greasy hat, a dirty face and an axe in his

4. In 1816 Charles Seabury was appointed missionary to the Episcopal congregations in Huntington and Islip, Long Island, in addition to his charge at Setauket.
During these years he generally officiated at his two mission charges once a month.

hand with which he appeared to have been hard at work—made towards us. "Wh-o-o," said my father to the horse—and in a moment I was convinced that before stood the redoubtable Mr. Saxon and an old broom handle at a short distance with a compass on the top of it was the instrument I had so eagerly coveted. In an instant my castle was in ruins! "Surveying!" I said to myself, "why I had as lieve[5] go back to the mahogany dust!"

I was now again completely on my back—and passed two or three days in a state of depression corresponding to the recent elation of my spirits. When the day came for my father's visit to Islip I had not much difficulty in persuading him to drive directly to the house of Mr. J. C. a N[ew] York merchant who had a county seat on the South Plains about six or eight miles from the church. My father knew that he would be here far more agreeably accommodated than he would in the cheerless tenement of the surveyor while I should escape the sight of a man whose image was at this moment as much an object of disgust as that of Moneygripe himself. Mr. C. had an elegant library. I gazed [at] it with admiration—and to this moment the titles of many of the books are fresh in my memory. On the top shelf almost out of sight lay a handsome copy of Virgil Delphini.[6] I opened it. It was all Latin—in a fair handsome type. I looked wistfully over pages. I called to mind the boys whom a few years before I had envied the task of reciting a lesson in it! I turned to the first book to find the words *arma virumque cano* which I had often read of as being the first verse of the celebrated poem.[7] I found the passage— looked at it attentively—but alass could make no sense of it! I closed the book saying to myself—two thousand years old! Written at Rome under Augutus Caesar! How venerable must it be! I opened it again and looked for the Georgics on which I remembered to have read in Echard that Virgil labored for seven years and on his death he

5. A dialect variation of *lief*, that is, gladly or willingly.
6. Seabury's script is blurred here, but he appears to be coining a unique figure of speech which praises Virgil as a poet inspired by Delphi itself.
7. "I sing of arms and the man," the first line of the first book of the *Aeneid*.

ordered them to be burned as an imperfect production.[8] I found
them comprised in a small compass. How perfect must they be! I
replaced the book—but an old train of feeling was reawakened not
soon to be extinguished. Before we left the house I requested my
father to borrow the book for me. He was somewhat surprised—but
readily consented. And this moment that I am writing the book
stands on my shelf—long the companion of my irregular studies and
the *nucleus* of a thousand associations. I was no sooner home than I
ran up into the study—tumbled over a pile of old books and among
them found the Latin Grammar which was the object of my search
and an old copy of Clarke's Justin—with the Latin in one column
and the English in the other.[9] This and the Virgil I laid carefully aside
for future use and immediately devoted myself to the study of the
Latin grammar. My father rather favored my pursuit than otherwise
supposing probably that without it I should be idle. He could however afford me no assistance. He had once indeed according to his
own record read as far as the third book of the Eneid but the *quae
omnia ruit vetustas* had obliterated almost every trace of classical
lore.[10] Occasionally indeed some faint recollection would be awakened. Once I remember (I anticipate my story for a moment) as the
Eneid was lying open before me, he looked over my shoulder and

8. The *Georgics* is a didactic poem in four books that deals with the subject of
agriculture. Seabury's request that his autobiographical sketch be burnt may perhaps
be a final Virgilian conceit, echoing the above.

9. Justinus was a Latin historian and epitomizer who was generally supposed to
have flourished in the age of the Antonines. His most famous work—*Historiarum
Philippicarum et Totius Mundi Originum, et Terrae Situs ex Trogo Pompeio Excerptarum
Libri XLIV a Nino ad Caesarem Augustum*—was a history of the world down to the
Roman conquest of the East. The edition of this work by John Clarke (1687–1734)
was a standard schoolboy's volume into the early nineteenth century since it provided
the Latin text along with a virtually literal translation. See Robert Middlekauff,
Ancients and Axioms: Secondary Education in Eighteenth Century New England (New
Haven: Yale University Press, 1963), 79–80.

10. "Old age which destroys all things." This may be a paraphrase of Ovid's
Metamorphoses, 15:234. *Eneid* was just a common variant spelling at the time of
Aeneid.

pointing to the clause *altae moenia Romae*[11] asked me to translate it. "The walls of lofty Rome," I replied. "Right my son," he rejoined. "I remember that old Dr. Mansfield used to get in a terrible fret with me sometimes for rendering it *the lofty walls of Rome.*"[12] At another time he pointed out to me the verse—*Infandum, regina [iubes renovare dolorem]*,[13] etc. and told me with great good humour the story of old President Styles having asked a mischievous young wag to translate it who exclaimed, "*Juves* you order me, *regina* o queen, *renovare* to change, *dolorem* a dollar, *infandum* to a pistorean."[14] It was on a similar occasion too that I first heard from him, in his own humorous way, of Dean Swift's odd translation of the line—*Romanos rerum dominos gentemque togatam.*[15] These were the only passages with which my father seemed to retain any acquaintance. But by agreeable conversation on the various authors of English literature interspersed with a variety of anecdote he considerably lightened my labors. But as I was saying in the downright drudgery of construction and literal translation he could yield me no facilities. He remembered however to have read Eutropius which he believed was the first book generally put into boys' hands and he knew there was such

11. *Aeneid* 1.7.

12. Richard Mansfield (1723–1820) was rector of the Hopkins Grammar School of New Haven until he converted to Anglicanism. Later he was also a minister in Derby, Connecticut, while continuing to teach Latin. He was elected by the Episcopal Church in Connecticut to act as an assistant bishop for Bishop Seabury, but was forced to refuse the honor because he could not afford the trip to England to secure consecration.

13. *Aeneid* 2.3, which properly translated should read, "Painful it is, O queen, for me to recount these things."

14. A pistorean was a Roman coin of small value. President Styles was probably Ezra Stiles, president of Yale College from 1778 to 1795.

15. *Aeneid* 1.282, which can be translated, "Romans, the togad nation, masters of all things." The allusion is to a story concerning Jonathan Swift recounted in Thomas Sheridan's *The Life of the Rev. Dr. Jonathan Swift* . . . (London, 1784). Annoyed by a large-nosed chaplain under the service of Lord Pembroke, Swift translated the passage "*Romanos*—you've a Roman nose—*rerum*—you're a rare rum—*dominos*—damn your nose—*gentemque togatam*, and the whole race of chaplains." See pp. 435–36.

a book as Clark's [*sic*] Eutropius.[16] I found it impossible to make sense of Justin and I therefore begged my father, who was now about preparing for his October visit to the city, to purchase for me Eutropius. This book he procured—a new handsome English copy—giving for it, by the bye, the identical dollar which I had received of Moneygripe and which had acquired in his hands such an adhesive power as to remain stationary till this moment in one corner of my trunk. I had by this time practiced so much in the Latin Grammar and on odd sentences that I found myself able on receiving the Eutropius to trace a tolerable degree of connexion between the Latin and the English. I now treated the pages of this iron-aged classic with all the nocturnal and diurnal manipulation which the most obsequious admirer of the Master of Lyric Poetry could bestow upon the illustrious authors of Greece.[17] One thing somewhat impeded my progress and that was the want of a portable dictionary—the one which I used being the huge quarto of Patrick's Ainsworth[18]—which was handled with difficulty and which being left about the room often furnished a topic of eloquent harrangue to Miss Sally Snarlingpan who was at present officiating as housekeeper. I could not think of asking my father to purchase a new dictionary—but I recollected having seen one in the neighborhood which I thought I could obtain. But the particulars and success of my application must be deferred to another chapter.

16. Eutropius was a Roman historian known primarily for his *Historia Romanae breviarum*. . . . John Clarke also did a standard edition of this work that was commonly used at the end of the eighteenth century.

17. Horace was usually considererd the master of lyric poetry. In his *Ars Poetica* (line 268) he writes, "For yourselves, handle Greek models by night, handle them by day."

18. Robert Ainsworth (1660–1748), *Thesaurus Linguae Latinae Compendarius: or a Compendious Dictionary of the Latin Tongue . . . Second Edition with Editions and Improvements by Samuel Patrick*. (London, 1746).

Seven

There are two sorts of individual character that are worth being studied and delineated. The one may be termed generic, the other anomalous. The former consists in a remarkable concentration of such features as distinguish generally a nation or strongly marked class of a community. The other is peculiar to the person possessing it. The one is commonly to be found under the feudal institutions of Europe or among the ancient peoples of the East and is seldom the growth of new and republican institutions. The other is occasionally met with in every part of the globe. The observation of the one is chiefly a source of improvement, that of the other rather of amusement. It is an anomaly of the latter description to which I am now about to introduce my readers: if they are averse to forming the acquaintance they may skip the chapter: though I venture to assure them that they will never again meet with the same odd amalgamation of eccentricities.

The day after our arrival at S[e]t[auke]t several of my father's new parishioners had assembled to assist him in the moving and arranging of his furniture. In the group he was one who though among them was not of them: being extremely officious and busying himself with the air of one who wished to obtain the *credit* of doing something rather than to *do* it. He could not escape notice. His dress was a swift colored great coat tied round his waist with a piece of list[1] and disclosing through its tatters what had once been [(]but probably on a former owner [)] a pair of *whole* pantaloons. He might have been forty-two or three years of age. He was rather tall and the little flesh that he had seemed to hang loose and flabby about his bones. His face

1. A narrow piece of cloth.

was long, narrow and full of wrinkles; white almost as chalk except two small spots of beard on his chin and upper lip. One eye was entirely blind—the pupil being overgrown with a sort of milky looking substance that had covered also about two-thirds of the other: so that all the power of vision the poor fellow had was by means of the third part of a single eye. As he moved among the articles of furniture around him he was obliged at every other step to twist his head and neck protruding his chin a little to the right so as to bring the remnant of his left eye to bear upon the spot his foot was about to cover. I have since thought that he would in some respects answer for the original of Homer's Thersites.[2] His name was Edward King—though for brevity's sake he was commonly termed Eddard. Among the moveables was a large trunk which two or three men were taking from a wagon. "A heavy, Eddard," said one of the men who had hold of it. "Eh," said Eddard, jerking his head to a right angle with his body so as to bring the chest within the point of his vision—"O no"—he continued in a squeaking womanish voice—"*it is not heavy—but it is a very bulky* a'ticle and is attracted by the 'a'th!"[3] This was spoken with an air of ineffable self conceit and produced as may be supposed a general laugh. For my own part though I had not learned the art of philosophizing upon character yet such a *lusus naturae*[4] as this could scarcely escape being an object of curiosity. From the neighbors I learned that he thought himself the richest and most learned man in the world—that he had been all his life time buying up the small stones that are found in clams and oysters which he believed to be pearls—making silver out of lead and gold out of stone—that his father once possessed a small property but had lost it by indulging Eddard in his chimerical pursuits. All this only stimulated my desire of further acquaintance, and it was

2. Thersites was an ugly, foul-tongued person who in the *Iliad* (2.212) rails against Agememnon until beaten by Odysseus.
3. That is, earth.
4. "Natural amusement."

not long ere I paid Eddard a visit. As I entered his residence—a miserable old hovel on a marsh at the head of a small cove which was washed away in a freshet a few years since, I beheld an old man who had nearly attained his ninetieth year seated straddled on a bench and cutting hoop roles with a drawing knife. This was the father of Eddard who worked at the coopering business and they both obtained their subsistence chiefly by the old man's labours though in a small part also by Eddard's hawking about the country a quantity of dry leaves which he very carefully cured every year which he believed himself and convinced some others to be the real tea plant. This he preferred himself to the choicest Imperial but as the old women in the neighborhood were obstinate in their preference for the cross-cut Bohea his sales were not very extensive.[5] I accosted the old man and asked if Eddard were in? *"Who's that wants me?"* was uttered in a squeaky voice from the only adjoining apartment. I turned my steps and in an instant beheld the object of my enquiry in the same immutable cloak which [was] his constant dress sleeping and waking, summer and winter—standing at a small cupboard—with a bone well stripped of its meat in one hand and in the other a pewter sauce pan nearly emptied of his delicious beverage. In one corner of the room were a couple of shelves covered with a few musty books—all which were the objects of Eddard's tenacious regard. Among them were two large volumes which were treasured with superstitious and peculiar veneration. These were Chamber's dictionary[6]—which in Eddard's estimation comprised the learning of the world. It was in vain that I used afterwards to assure him that there were several Encyclopedias published since Chamber's time that were far more valuable depositories of knowledge. All that was good in them he averred had been stolen from Chambers—and

5. Bohea was a fine quality Chinese black tea, and Imperial was that Chinese tea known as the "perfection of tea."

6. Ephraim Chambers (c. 1680–1740), *Cyclopaedia: or An Universal Dictionary of Arts and Sciences* (London, 1728). Seabury's spelling of the name is inconsistent.

everything else was trash. The books had formerly belonged to Dr. Penderson a physician of the place and at his demise had been taken by Eddard's father in payment of a debt. Both were unable to read, but persons were found kind enough to perform the service for them: and the illumination which by this means overflooded the genius of the son was the means of reducing them both to their present state of poverty. But I am detaining the reader from the dialogue to which my entrance gave rise.

"Good morning Eddard."

"Good morning sir, good morning. How do you do?"

"Quite well thank you."

"Your Pappy well and your Mammy?"[7]

"Very well."

"Well that's clever—I consider health the greatest blessing a man can have. What do *you* think?" He began thus as all his sentences with a powerful impetus on the first part of it and pointed off the latter part with a most inimitable squeek. "I believe it is the first—and next to that riches." "Well now there we differ. I don't consider riches in itself to be any blessing at all." "No—they are not valuable in themselves—but as the means of procuring other comforts." "Other comforts! God—that would make them valuable enough. But sometimes they a'n't good for that. Why young man I've got riches enough to buy all Long Island—yes—half the state of N[ew] Y[ork] and yet you see what I am with hardly enough to eat or drink."

"Why Eddard I've heard people talk—" "Talk? I suppose you don't believe me—but the pearls alone in this old room are worth millions of money. The largest pearl in Europe formerly belonged to the Emperor of France and now belongs to the Emperor of Rushy [Russia]—and that only weighs (he mentioned the weight to half a

---

7. The reference to Seabury's mother suggests that this conversation in all likelihood took place in 1814–15 before Seabury's apprenticeship.

penny weight)—and I can show you five that weighs more than double."

"But Eddard why don't you dispose of one or two of them?"

"Why who'll buy them? There's nobody in this country that knows the valey on 'em. All a set of butchers and cobblers. If I could get to the foreign powers I'd sell 'em quick enough—I have been to all the Counsuls in N[ew] Y[ork]—but they're a set of ignorant fellows and don't understand the interests of their courts at all—the British Counsul told me once that he had sent out a speciman that I gave him—and that the Court of Great Britain did not want them—but he is a lying, cheating rascal—and I told him so to his face—they know the valley [*sic*] of these things better in that country."

"But the N[ew] Y[ork] jewellers know the value of silver—why don't you sell some of that to them?"

"Why I'll tell you. I took one bar of silver (he kept it in small bars about six inches long) which I had been more than a month refining from forty lbs. of le[a]d and three of zinc and I took it to them that called themselves the first rate jewellers in York and they had the impudence to tell me it was no'ink but pewter. Now what's a man to do with such ignorant lying rascals as them be?"

"Nothing but pewter, eh? Well maybe they were right?"

"Right! God o' massy! Doesn't every philosophy know that lead had a *residuum* of silver? and don't the zinc being a harder metal similize with the residuum and make it consisty? And didn't I work at it for twenty years before I brought the art to perfection?"

"Well but Mr. King (for so it was prudent to accost him when his temper was ruffled) where did you learn this art?"

"Out of Chamber's Dictionary—the only book in the world of true learning."[8]

"Don't you suppose that other people read Chambers besides you?"

---

8. Chambers (1:57) includes an article on "alchymy" which defines it as "a higher or more refined kind of Chymistry, employed in the more mysterious Researches of the Art." Chambers, however, does not include any instructions.

"Well, sir, they've got to be very scarce—there isn't another to be found in this country—besides, young man, it isn't every body that reads Chambers that has the *genus* to see into the secrets of alkeemy."

"Why Mr. King don't you know that the science of alchymy has long since been exploded from the world?"

"Be sure I do: and I know the world 'd be divilish glad to get it back again if it could. He e e!"

"Well, Eddard, they tell me that you possess considerable gold?"

"Well not exactly—I have some—but no great quantity—I haven't quite brought that art to perfection. I hope to accomplish it one of these days. Here's some stone that I shall begin to purify in a short time. You may see the gold in 'em if you look—but it's not so easy to get it out as you may think for."

He pointed me to a pile of sand stone in one corner with some bright yellow specks in it. I looked at it—wished him success and begged him to show me his pearls. "No, no, young man, it is not every body I show my pearls to"—and indeed it was only twice in all my intercourse with this oddity that I obtained sight of the blue dingy excrescencies which he so highly prized. On them and indeed on all his treasures he used to gaze with infinite delight: and when he displayed them he held the box that contained them firmly in both hands twisting his head about in every direction so as to bring each one within the angle of his vision. Indeed the infinite self-complacency with which, in the extreme of ignorance and poverty, he exulted in the conscious possession of wealth and knowledge would have reminded a moral anatomist of that wise process of compensation by which the benificent author of nature so often atones for deficiencies of one kind by bestowing benefits of another.

It was on the shelves of this singular creature that I had observed an old Latin dictionary which wanted but few pages of being whole and was otherwise in a tolerable state of preservation. How to obtain it was the difficulty: for [as] much as Eddard coveted money he considered it, like many other admirers of learning, mere trash in comparison with his books. An expedient at length occurred to me which proved amply successful. I had in my possession a beautiful piece of crystallized quartz [(]which had been given me, when an infant, for a plaything[)]—about as long as my finger and of perfect shape and transparency. With this in my pocket I went to the abode of the one-eyed Mercury and after much difficulty prevailed on him to show me his diamonds.[9] Opening a small trap door he brought out a chest with much ado whence he took a small box containing several pieces of rock crystal. These he held before me performing as usual such a variety of evolutions with his head and neck that a stranger would have put him down for a confirmed victim of St. Vitus's dance.[10] "Do you call these diamonds, Eddard?" I asked in rather a contemptuous tone. "These are the rale ginooine," he replied, "equal to any of the great Mogools." "Well," said I, "if these are diamonds what do you think of this?" Thus saying, I took the crystal out of my pocket and held it steadily before his face. Never did I behold such an expression. He threw his head back slightly twisting his neck so that his nose need not intercept the object of his wonder—and then with both hands uplifted and his mouth wide open he exclaimed, with a most distinct enunciation, while his shrill voice was elevated to a shriek: "*O good God!*" He seized hold of the crystal—carried it to the window and stooping down so as to bring it between the light and the fraction of his optical orb—continued to exclaim "G'acious heaven! God of majesty! why, where? Daddy, Daddy! do come here! By jolly! *Why where did you get this?*"

9. Mercury, or Hermes the "thrice greatest," was known in the ancient world as the revealer of magical and mystical knowledge including alchemy. Thus to later generations he became known as the source of the hidden, or hermetic, traditions of knowledge.

10. Vitus was a Sicilian youth, believed to be patron of actors, dancers, and those who found it difficult to rise in the morning. In sixteenth-century Germany it was believed that good health could be secured by dancing before a statue of the saint on his feast day. The ecstatic dance later became associated with the disease of chorea.

I will only add that I left the gewgaw[11] with Eddard and obtained in exchange the dictionary accompanied with a thousand thanks and indeed I believe I might have bartered it for Chambers himself. I shall now return to my narrative leaving my readers, I hope not displeased at their introduction to so eccentric a character as an alchymist of the nineteenth century.

11. That is, something lacking in substantial value.

Eight

This volume[1] being much more easy of reference than the ponderous quarto which I had previously used materially facilitated my progress: and had it not been for one circumstance I should now have been as happy in the pursuit of knowledge as the visionary Eddard himself could have been in search of the philosopher's stone.[2] There *was* one circumstance however that was a source of annoyance and that was my dependance on my father for boarding and clothes of one of which certainly and perhaps of both I knew he would have been relieved by my continuance at Moneygripe's. In order to remove this embarrassment I proposed to my father (of course without hinting to him my real nature) that I should take a few boys from the neighborhood to instruct during the winter. My father with his usual good nature sanctioned the project adding that it would afford me employment and could do no harm. No time was lost in announcing the plan to the neighbors and on the first of November 1816 about eight o'clock in the morning in an unfinished room on the second floor of our dwelling I was awaiting, in magisterial dignity, the arrival of those children whose parents might condescend to honor me with their patronage. I know not whether it was from the contempt in which Mr. Leadenfrate, the then incumbent of the district school was held, or from my own reputation for mathematical skill (for it was well known that I had ciphered through the arithmetic and it was even rumored that I understood Surveying and Navigation) but certain it is that in the course of a week after I

1. A reference to the Latin dictionary mentioned in letter seven.
2. The philosopher's stone was a substance that according to some alchemists would convert all base metals into gold. The search for such a stone was a traditional quest for alchemy.

had thrown open my doors I remembered rising twenty pupils and among these three or four of the largest boys of the village and one who had been long reputed to be the best *cipherer* of his school. It may well be supposed that success so exceeding my expectations stimulated my exertions; while the difficulty of maintaining authority over a hale young peasantry, more than one of whom, had it come to the question of physical strength, could have pitched me out of the window, called for no little adroitness. My efforts however were unwearied. The younger classes I drilled fruitfully in reading and spelling endeavoring to the best of my ability to break of their rustic habits of pronunciation while the remainder I assisted, with some success that, before the close of winter, the most difficult sums of Daboll's Arithmetic were recorded on the pages of their respective ciphering books.[3] Not content with this I formed the noble plan of teaching one of them, who was the most advanced, Algebra, a science of which the very name had never before been heard by any under my tutelage. To be sure at the time I opened my school I was myself totally ignorant of the science: or at least only had a vague notion that, by some mysterious process, results were obtained by *letters* instead of *figures*. Thinking, however, that I might surprise my scholars and urged on by my own intense curiosity I determined, if possible, to get some insight into this wonderful branch of knowledge. I referred to the article in the Encyclopedia and after reading a few pages found, to my inexpressible joy, that I could understand it. I now devoted myself to this alluring study with intense application and in the course of a short time was enabled to obtain the results of all the sums in single and double position together with a number of others by an algebraical process. I am sure that the most obdurate Stoic would have pardoned the luxurious feeling of gratified pride with which I paraded to my admiring pupils the new stock of mysterious knowledge which now raised my fame among them to the

3. Nathan Daboll (1750–1818), *Daboll's Schoolmaster's Assistant. Being a Plain Practical System of Arithmetic. . . .* First published in 1799.

very zenith of its glory. I was much surprised, however, to find that though I explained to them one or two formulas with all the clearness imaginable, they could not understand me and the most incredulous among them ventured to throw out the suspicion that I was hoaxing them having previously obtained the results by means of figures. One of them however was disposed to make the subject a formal study and I accordingly undertook to instruct him: taking good care as may be imagined to make him serve a due course of apprenticeship at Addition and the other fundamental rules before I initiated him into the *Ultima Thule*[4] of my own acquirements—the mystery of simple equations.

All this time my Latin was not entirely neglected. I had read Eutropius through three times and had made some progress in Justin: devoting to my studies (in which I must include the puzzling which I was frequently put to, to solve the more difficult problems in advance of my class and which I looked out for with as much anxiety as a mariner would for breakers ahead) all the time which could be spared from my necessary avocation and the duties of my school. As the spring opened my pupils began to return to the plough and on the first of May my father changed his residence and the school was disbanded. And now succeeded a breathing spell of about two months in which I had nothing else to do but thumb the leaves of my grammar and dictionary. The latter of these books not withstanding my use of a translation was as pertinaciously consulted as it would have been in the hands of the most drudging school boy: for my pride would not suffer me to avail myself more than possible of any short cuts to learning and I was always stiffly resolved to regard my translation simply as in lieu of a teacher, referring to it only or chiefly to confirm or correct my own previous interpretation of a passage. In the course of this interim I had read through Justin (without

4. Farthest Thule. The phrase is from Virgil's *Georgics*, 1:30. In the ancient world, Thule was believed to be the northernmost part of the inhabited world, and it came to symbolize any distant, mysterious, or mythical region, or metaphorically a remote goal or end.

however having the patience to revise him) and had plodded through a whole book of that divine poem of Virgil's [*sic*] which has so long been

the theme of wisdom and the sport of fools.

My mind however again began to be perplexed with doubts as to the future direction of my conduct. Sometimes I flattered myself with the hope that by persevering a while longer I might become capable of assisting at a school in the great city of New York: while at others I became a reluctant convert to the passive philosophy of my father that something favorable probably would turn up or at any rate that providence would overrule all things for the best.

In this state of suspense as my father and myself were one day passing through an old orchard, in the rear of the house, on our return from a ramble through the fields, the old gentleman suddenly starting exclaimed with one of those ejaculations which were the remnants of his hereditary loyalty, "Bless the King! Sam, but I had like to have forgot that I received, yesterday morning, a letter from your aunt in which you are somewhat concerned."[5] This aunt, to whom I have before had occasion to allude, had on the first of May resumed a charge, which had for some years been suspended on account of ill health, and taken a few young ladies under her care for tuition.[6] I waited with the most eager impatience while my father, with the utmost deliberation, taking out his pocket handkerchief, and wiping the perspiration from his face and exclaiming, "My stars and garters how warm it is!" proceeded in due form to produce the letter and read part of its contents. It contained, as the reader may anticipate, a proposal from my aunt that, until some more eligible

5. Both Seabury's father and grandfather had been strong Tories during the period of the Revolutionary War. See the Introduction.

6. It is uncertain which aunt this was. The New York City directory of 1816 lists an Eliza Seabury as a teacher, but Eliza Seabury is not included in the Seabury genealogy. According to the compiler of the genealogy (William J. Seabury, son of Samuel) this aunt was either Violetta, Abigail Mumford, or Mary.

situation presented itself, I should make her house my home and assist her in the labors of her school. "Tell him that my means are small"—said my father continuing to read the letter—"but he shall eat of my bread and drink of my cup!" My father very composedly folded up the letter and began to discourse on its contents in the same probing style in which he was used to discuss a text from the pulpit. But my imagination had already levied the proposal with avidity and in less than a week I again returned to the city of Knickerbocker in a far different frame of mind from that in which I had abandoned the premises of Moneygripe. Previously to going however I made out the accounts of my last winter's tuition and left them with my father: for although in this humble station, I had labored with the utmost fidelity, yet the consciousness of my youth and the fear of being taxed with presumption for having undertaken so important a charge, so dampened my resolution that I could not bring myself to present my bills for settlement nor indeed had I ever afterwards courage to enquire of my father after their fate.

Nine

I do not remember ever to have been much interested in any person whom I had never seen without forming to myself a picture more or less vivid of his features, dress and general appearance. Nor do I believe myself singular in this respect. The most etherial [*sic*] brain that ever was buoyed up above the clouds of physics into that metaphysical region so difficult of respiration was never so in love with abstractions as not to give figure and coloring at least to the subjects of biography and history and romance too if he ever condescended to read it. Such a person would be *meta*physical indeed— utterly out of the range of our common nature. Every reader, I doubt not, keeps one department of his imagination as a picture gallery: where portraits of heroes of all sorts, real and fictitious, handsome and deformed, are hung up for his occasional amusement. But fancy sometimes plays strange freaks: and often it happens that after having invested an unknown with all material attributes, we are woefully disappointed to find the ideal picture as unlike as possible to the reality. Now lest when I inform the reader, that in the commencement of my seventeenth year, that most sensitive period of human life, I was about to be introduced, in the capacity of usher,[1] to a number of young ladies—at least some of whom, it must be supposed, were fast ranging towards the corresponding period of sensibility which it is the happy privilege of their sex to anticipate, he should forthwith invest me with the prepossessing aspect of the florid and agreeable bean or the pensive and retiring student of romance, performing an apotheosis on every beauty that he meets, I deem it advisable to give him some little outline of my

1. That is, an assistant teacher.

general appearance even at the risque of diminishing his interest in the narrative of my fortunes. I must tell him then in a word that instead of possessing any of those captivating qualities which have inveighed similar situations with hidden dangers and have led to premature and proscribed engagements or even to a runaway match I was a tall, gawky, overgrown sickly looking boy: such an utter stranger to all the usual topics of interest to the sexes that there was scarce a girl of twelve years of age from whom I could not have taken a lesson and not a boy of her own age whom she would not have found a more apt scholar. Perhaps this was owing partly to constitutional apathy, increased by a sedentary habit quite unnatural to my time of life, but it was more to be attributed to the affected Stoicism of my philosophy and the real devotional admiration with which I contemplated the pious austerity of St. Basil and all the holy anchorites.[2] I was moreover the last person in the world that in regard to personal appearance would even have thought of atoning for the deficiency of natural grace by the trickery of artificial show. This will be believed when I have given a brief outline of my dress at this auspicious era of my life. My feet—so long and sprawling as always to be an object of particular observation—were covered with a pair of substantial thick soled cow hide shoes—without binding and so long without blacking as to have lost the original stock they received from the tanner. My coat and pantaloons—which were of course grey cloth—had become quite too small for me owing to the rapidity of my growth; the latter not reaching to my ankles and the former being of such rational dimensions that I had not then as I have ever since the trouble of moving the lappells [sic] (or skirts I believe I should call them) every time I was disposed to sit down. My hat too which had become rounded at the top and quite peaked,

2. St. Basil the Great (A.D. c. 330–379) was one of the Cappadocian fathers of the Greek church. He was also known as the organizer of eastern monasticism and ranks with St. Benedict in the history of Christian monachism. Anchorites were monks who withdrew from the world to live a solitary life of silence, prayer, and mortification.

owing to my *capital* expansion, caused me as I stood bolt upright to present an object which (if I may be pardoned the hyperbole) an army of liliputians would have taken for a liberty pole.[3] My aunt gave me, "accoutered as I was" a welcome reception though she did not fail soon to suggest (a motion in which my father readily acquiesced though no more than myself would he ever have thought of it) that I should make an early visit to the hatter, the shoemaker and the tailor adding with a sarcastic spirit that she could never suppress, as she looked at my long, stiff unbrushed hair, that though I had little marks of *civilization* to spare she would nevertheless recommend me to be *barbarized*.

Sufficient change being thus wrought in my externals to prevent my coming an object of merriment or wonder to my airy pupils, I was forthwith inducted into the duties of my office. Every morning before the hours of school I was employed in making pens and ruling copybooks and, during the hours of school, in hearing recitations of English Grammar and Geography and endeavoring, with all mathematical sobriety, to transfuse a knowledge of figures into some of the giddiest brains that ever winced under the curbs and bits[4] of an abstract science. The peculiar repugnance and sometimes the presumptuous contempt which were evinced by the tenants of a fairy realm for the divine art of Pythagorus[5] were far from raising them (at that period I mean) in my estimation and effectually shielded me from all such shafts as might have impaired my devotion to the venerable relics of antiquity. All the time that I could spare was assiduously devoted to the acquisition of Latin verbiage, which I had by this time learned to invest with a perfection that belonged to no other language upon earth. I procured a copy of Caesar's Commentaries, without notes and wretchedly printed, and read through the

3. Lilliput was the first country mentioned in Jonathan Swift's *Gulliver's Travel*, in which the inhabitants were one-twelfth human size.
4. Curbs and bits were used in riding horses.
5. That is, mathematics.

Gallic and civil wars;[6] with an interest in the latter somewhat above
that of mere translation but with a stupid indifference to the history
of the former (except in the sixth book) which I have never been able
entirely to overcome.[7] Mair's Introduction, too, was faithfully studied[8] and on the arrival to the city it had been one of my first acts to go
to a certain Episcopal bookstore, whither my father was in the habit
of carrying me, and enquire for a key.[9] The reader must call to mind
my strong feelings of pride and bashfulness and that stiffness of
manner which I then possessed utterly at variance with the easy
lubricity with which something of this world's polish has since enabled me to escape from the little discomfitures of life, in order to
appreciate the effect of an affront (unintentional as I believe most
others have been that I have received) to which I was exposed in
procuring the last mentioned book. Every body knows *the oracle* that
at this Delphos of Episcopacy so eloquently delivers his opinions on
all matters of interest to the church. It was to him that I signified my
wish to purchase a copy of the Key to Mair's Introduction. "We have
the book, sir," he replied with his usual flippancy, "but it would be
impossible for us to sell you a copy, as we consider ourselves bound
in honor, not to part with it except to teachers or professors." I was
about departing in a state of absolute suffocation when Mr. J. U.
with a characteristic trick of the trade, laying down the paper which

6. *De Bello Gallico* and *De Bello Civili.*

7. In the sixth book of the Gallic Wars Caesar gives an account of the customs of
the Gauls, Germans, and Druids as well as describing a punitive raid against the
Eburones and their leader Ambiorix.

8. John Mair (1702/3–1769), *An Introduction to Latin Syntax: or An Exemplification
of the Rules of Construction, as Delivered in Mr. Ruddiman's Rudiments . . . Revised,
Corrected and Enlarged by George Ironside* (New York, 1813).

9. Most probably Thomas and James Swords' bookstore at No. 160 Pearl Street in
New York. The Swords were the main publishers for the Episcopal Church in New
York during the early nineteenth century and their bookstore was a meeting place for
the clergy of New York City and vicinity. They were also the publishers of Mair's
Introduction. See Clifford P. Morehouse, "Almanacs and Yearbooks of the Episcopal
Church, "*Historical Magazine of the Protestant Episcopal Church* 10 (1941): 332–33.

he was reading, said "O I guess you may venture to let Mr. S[ea-bury] take one!" and fearing that I should not obtain one elsewhere on easier terms I paid my money and departed. The book was of essential service to me as I had the patience to write down almost the whole of the Introduction comparing every lesson, for correction, as soon as it was finished with the Key. If there were any differences between my own exercises and the Key in which I could not see the reasons of preference to the latter I used carefully to note their recurrence and by the collation of several such instances in various passages, generally succeeded in discovering the true principle at issue.

My time thus passed on without much variety. The chief current of my mind was its Latin devotion: though even this was subject to its ebbs and flows; as I was sometimes in a state of despondency and at others very sanguine of success. In these states of depression I would sometimes read one of the Waverlies (which were just then beginning to attract attention)[10] or some fugitive reading (with which my aunt being the subscriber of a circulating library was generally supplied), or I would play a game of chess with my uncle who resided at a short distance. I shrank instinctively from everything like cultivation of acquaintances and had not an intimate of my own age in the world. Besides Latin I had no other regular study unless the repeated but fitful efforts which I made to obtain a skill in English composition may be dignified with that title. I had read Dr. Franklin's life and was in the habit of trying the plan which he recommends of reading some article in the Spectator and then writing down the ideas from memory.[11] But whether it was from any defect in the plan itself or that my understanding was not yet sufficiently improved to be benefitted by it I know not, but I certainly cannot boast of deriving from it either pleasure or profit and not once, in the highest inebriation of vanity, was I ever able to discover

10. The Waverlies were thirty-two novels and tales written by Sir Walter Scott, which began appearing in 1814.

11. See *The Autobiography of Benjamin Franklin*, ed. Leonard W. Labaree, et al. (New Haven: Yale University Press, 1964), 61–62.

that I improved upon my author. Another expedient which I shall have occasion presently to mention was of more service. There were also two or three of Horace's odes[12] which in the winter of 1817 I turned into a sort of kangaroo rhyme. To be sure I had to delve a long time for the literal meaning before I could harness it in the chains of English verse: but then, in mitigation it should be known, that the Horace I had was the mere text and that as I afterwards discovered filled with the most egregious typographical errors. In the Spring of the following year (1818) I applied myself to the Greek Grammar and by the month of June thought myself prepared to commence the translation of the testament, recollecting enough of the process which I had observed at the last school I went to, to know that I must begin with St. John's gospel. The strangeness of the Greek characters which is a fright to some beginners had no terrors for me as, being prompted by a feeling which according to the best of my recollections might have been analyzed into equal parts of curiosity and vanity, I had familiarized my eye to them before I was eleven years of age by learning the alphabet in an old Greek Grammar which was among my father's books. But there was another difficulty rather more annoying though of a similiar kind. The only copy of the testament which I had (and I had no money to spare for the purchase of another) was filled with abbreviations: this however was easily surmounted by reading over the genealogical record in St. Matthew and Luke[13] and comparing the Greek names with those in the English translation. Thus disciplined with the help of the English translation and a Dawson's Lexicon, I had by the month of July read through the gospels and the Acts.[14] I mean to say in so many words that I accomplished this task in the course of one month: rising at five o'clock in the morning and devoting to it every moment I could

12. Horace (Quintius Horatius Flaccus) had a four book collection of odes or carminas.

13. Matthew 1:1–17 and Luke 3:23–38

14. Joannes Dawson, *Lexicon Novi Testimenti Alphabeticum* was originally published in London in 1702.

command until ten at night. But having said this I must add what will destroy the wonder of the feat and that is that on the whole it was the most slovenly, shuffling piece of study that I ever performed. To be sure I could have opened a Greek Testament any where that I had read and hit something like the sense of it in English—but then the accuracies of grammar were so wholly neglected that I doubt whether in two instances out of the three I could have distinguished a first aorist tense from a second.[15]

About the end of July 1818 my father made a visit to the city and seemed to listen with satisfaction to the account I gave him of my proficiency. He enquired into my ultimate plans and I mentioned the ministry as the object of my hopes: being now satisfied that the greatest apparent obstacles—the acquisition of the dead languages was not insurmountable. So far from making any opposition he now began to devise means by which the attainment of the object could be facilitated. A friend of his resided a few miles from the city who is well known to the public as combining the character of the amiable gentleman, the accomplished scholar and the dignified Christian. My father proposed a visit to the abode of this reverend patron of the arts in order that my literary acquisitions might be subjected to a critical examination. Thither we accordingly went and I well remember the surprise I felt on entering a library which for display in elegant and sacred literature surpassed all I had ever seen. Dr. J.——— gave us a very polite and friendly reception and undertook in a very gentlemanly way to perform the favor which my father had solicited. He asked me what books I had read in Latin? I replied Eutropius, Justin, a few books of the Eneid, Caesar's Commentaries, Sallust and the first volumes of Pliny's natural history.[16]

15. The tense of verb denoting that an action or occurrence took place in a past time without implication of continuance or repetition. First and second aorist, though having the same meaning, are formed quite differently.

16. Sallust was a Roman historian who among other things was the author of a history of the Cataline conspiracy *Bellum Catalinae*. Pliny the Elder was the author of *Historia Naturalis*.

Letter Nine

He took from the shelf a resplendent copy of Virgil and opening at the beautiful passage of which Rollin has given us so critical an analysis—Vix e conspictu Siculae, etc., requested me to read and translate it.[17] There was something in his manners which gave me complete self possession and enabled me to perform the requisition with justice to myself. Alive as he was to the beauties of polite literature I think his ears must have received no common outrage at my uncouth and barbarous pronunciations. This was a defect however which he had sense enough to excuse though I much query whether could he have looked within my mind, he would have regarded with similar generosity the indifference bordering on contempt with which in the self-sufficiency of conceited ignorance I listened to the easy and mellifluous enuciations with which he redeemed the passage from the murder that had just been perpetrated on it. He thus enquired into the state of my Greek and understanding that I had read the gospels and the Acts turned to a chapter in the latter and examined me with such delicacy as to leave me under the impression that I had stood the ordeal in a very satisfactory manner. He was lavish with his praises and as seventeen is about the vainest period of human life it will not be wondered at when I say that the soil of my mind was light and sandy enough to absorb the whole of them. To my father too he expressed himself highly pleased and offered to do, whatever was in his power, to further my wishes. He gave me a letter of introduction to a literary operative in the city and understanding from my father that pecuniary embarrassment alone had prevented him from gratifying my desire of a liberal education very promptly made him an offer from his own resources which would in part remove the difficulty. In the course of my Greek examination he mentioned with some surprise a coincidence which I have since been more capable of appreciating and have thought at least singular. In answer to some question in regard to the Greek

17. *Aeneid* 1.34, "hardly out of sight of Sicilian land. . . ." Charles Rollin (1661–1741) discussed this passage in *The Method of Teaching and Studying the Belles Lettres . . . Translated from the French*, 4 vols. (London, 1742), 1:270–72.

article I told him that I had been in the habit of considering it not simply an article as the Grammar called it but rather as a relative pronoun and preferred to parse and translate it accordingly. Thus was I unconsciously and as it were instinctively acting on a doctrine to the establishment of which Bishop Middleton has brought such varied and extensive learning and deep metaphysical research.[18]

Dr. J. had encouraged my father to believe that I could yet obtain the benefits of a collegiate education. He told him of a Society[19] in the city instituted for the purpose of aiding young men in indigent circumstances who were looking towards the ministry and from which he had no doubt I could obtain pecuniary assistance and this together with the facility he had himself offered and such contributions as my friends could add (for in this *pauper-like* style I was talked of) would be sufficient it was thought to defray my expenses. How nearly I was qualified to enter college he would not decide but referred us for information on such points to the gentleman in the city to whom he had given us a letter of introduction. Accordingly on the next day we waited on M. N. by whom it was proposed I should again be examined.[20] N. was a regular pedagogue, combining in full proportions, all the vain, conceited, dogmatical and terrific ingredients that enter into the concoction of that preposterous character. He gave me the animated passage *His animum arrecti dictis*, etc., as a trial of my skill.[21] I began: but the grove of Apollo and the laboratory of Vulcan were different places; and the self possession which

18. Thomas Middleton (1769–1822), first bishop of Calcutta, in 1808 published *The Doctrine of the Greek Article Applied to the Criticism and Illustration of the New Testament* in which he used his interpretation of the biblical Greek to buttress the biblical evidence for the divinity of Jesus.

19. The Protestant Episcopal Society for the Promotion of Religion and Learning in the State of New York.

20. This examiner could possibly have been Nathaniel F. Moore (1782–1872) who was both adjunct professor of classics at Columbia College (and much later to serve successively as full professor, librarian, and president) and also, as nephew of the late Bishop Benjamin Moore, was involved in the life of the Episcopal Church in New York.

21. *Aeneid* 1.579, "Stirred in spirit by these words."

had sustained me the day before in the former, now completely forsook me in the latter. I hurried through the part assigned me in a state of mental confusion and trepidation rendering it tolerably well till I came to the words *dictis respondent coetera matris;*[22] the construction of which I did not at the moment perceive and adopted the school boy expedient of slurring them over with a hasty and obscure translation. But this was no time for official vigilance to be napping: and N. quick as lightning asked me to repeat my translation of the passage. An instant's recollection however brought me to my senses and I rendered it correctly. The result of our interview was an assurance that I was prepared for college in my Latin studies and that if I could receive a dispensation from the faculty for my deficiencies in Greek I should probably be able to make them [up] in the course of the first session.

Thus the fact of my being qualified for college was established and the pecuniary obstacles to so desirable a destiny were in a fair way of being removed. But such are the fluctuations of human nature that what two or three years before I would have coveted as the greatest good upon earth was now an object of indifference and almost aversion. This change, however, in my mind was by no means the result of caprice. On the contrary there were several considerations any one of which would have been in my mind an invincible objection to the plan proposed and which all together fully determined me to decline all the facilities towards its accomplishment which my friends might offer. The first objection was an instinctive repugnance to pecuniary obligation. The offer of Dr. J. I could not be prevailed on to accept. And I may here be permitted to record with a feeling of satisfaction that with one exception I have never received an obligation of this kind towards the advancement of my studies. The exception alluded to was two years after the time I am now speaking of: when, in order to gratify my father, who after unwearied pains had succeeded in obtaining a grant of $100 per an[num] from the Society

22. Line 585, "all else agrees with thy mother's words."

above named, I was induced for once to accept it—but soon after requested my name to be stricken from the Society's books. The other objection to the college project was the consciousness of an awkwardness of manner which I had acquired by my seclusion from Society and a natural dislike which I felt for mingling in the company of boys three or four [years] younger than myself; and above all the horror I felt in consequence of my disadvantages of appearing among them as an inferior.

These considerations, especially perhaps the last decided me against any attempt at going to college, and after two or three visits to Mr. N———— I soon relapsed into my recluse and unsocial habits. At one of these visits I was introduced to Mr. W————[23] whose acquaintance a year or two subsequent was resumed: besides which nothing happened that had the least influence on my mind or conduct; for though I was then in the habit of writing Latin compositions I had never the courage to offer one of them to N's inspection nor to ask of him any sort of literary assistance. The same diffidence deterred me from accepting an invitation from Dr. J. to spend a week in his family and though I do not remember to have seen him since yet I cannot but hope that the opportunity will occur to me of personally assuring him that the recollection of his kindness at that period has never been obliterated. Nothing else that I remember happened to vary the monotony of my life until in the fall of this year my aunt was compelled from the decline of health to break up her school. The change in my circumstances which was thus effected shall be related in the chapter following.

23. This may be the same individual referred to later as Mr. Brouse. (See below, page 125.)

Ten

I am not yet so thorough a convert to the new school of poetry as not to admire Mr. Pope[1] as a true poet as well as the most finished versifier of the language; and thus too maugre[2] a number of nonsensical couplets in his Herculean translation and a few paradoxes that are the product of Bolingbroke's philosophy.[3] One of these latter blemishes is a passage in the Universal Prayer which I have often heard selected as a peculiar corruscation[4] of profound genius but which appears to me to be as elaborate nonsense as was ever distilled from a metaphysical brain. If either the poet himself or his philosophical master or his paradoxical commentator attached any clear conception of human agency or divine to the hemistich

> And binding all things fast in fate
> left free the human will[5]

tis pity that for the benefit of inferior mortals they had not left explanations on record. But what sort of freedom is a man to exercise when all events past, present and future are fixed? What freedom can there be without contingency? How can every individual will be free while yet it has nothing to do, nothing to avoid, nothing

1. A reference to the literary clash between the new school of Romantic poetry and the older neoclassicism as represented by its most accomplished proponent Alexander Pope.

2. This is an archaic expression meaning in spite of, or notwithstanding.

3. Henry St. John, Viscount Bolingbroke (1678–1751) was notorious for his Deistic beliefs. His influence has been noted in Pope's poem, "Universal Prayer."

4. That is, coruscation or a brilliant flash of wit.

5. This hemistich, or half line of verse, from "Universal Prayer" was evidently quoted from memory since what Pope wrote was "And binding Nature fast in Fate / Left free the human Will" (lines 11–12).

to direct, nothing to control? For certainly if all things are bound fast in fate, there is nothing which can be either a positive or negative result of the human will.[6] That there are events in the economy of Providence that are fixed and may thus be said to be bound in *fate*— taking the word in its best and literal sense for the determined and *declared* counsel of God and that such a fate is consistent with a limited freedom of the human will, in other words with moral agency, is sound philosophy and theology: and if Mr. P[ope] had succeeded in condensing this truth in a short poetical aphorism he would have deserved the thanks of posterity. In relation to these great events our individual wills are the winds in the cavern of Aeolus; our energies may struggle and our passions roar: they will but rage around the barriers of determinate counsel while the Supreme Ruler restrains them with authority and binds them with the chains and in the prison of destiny.

> Luctantis ventos tempestatesque sonoras
> Imperio premit ac vinclis et carcere frenat.
> Illi indignantes magno cum murmure montis
> Circum claustra fremunt.[7]

But the human wills of Mr. Pope without power over the smallest contingency but with *all things* bound fast about them are the adverse winds in the battle of Ulysses

> Securely fettered by a silver thong

the most tame insipid things imaginable; while his Providence instead of controlling the operations of human agency by the majestic barriers of omnipotence may be pictured as holding in his hand a bag

6. In the text the line"Such free wills are the winds in the cavern of Aeolus" has been crossed out.

7. Aeolus was ruler of the winds. In the *Aeneid* he is portrayed as keeping the winds in a cave on Aeolia. The passage cited in the above text was from 1:53 ff., "[Aeolus] keeps under his sway and with his prison bonds curbs the struggling winds and roaring gales."

of goatskin![8] That small and great events appear to us to be woven in the same web is surely no reason for believing that they were from all eternity bound up in necessary connexion. It reflects far more dignity on the character and on the attributes of God to believe that there are many and great events which man is free to control and many more which God, in perfect consistency with his great ultimate designs, has reserved to himself the power, in his providence over human life of alloting to his creatures according to the varying exigencies of their state and character. On no other philosophical grounds would it seem possible to defend that highest characteristic of a great mind—the determination not [to] be *passive* under events but to *control* them:—not to yield to them but to make them bend to itself. And it is no small confirmation of the truth of our creed that this inflexible determination is often found to triumph over the most adverse circumstances.

I fear the reader will be fatigued by this digression: but as I am writing for my own edification as well as his amusement I shall find it necessary, every once in a while, to take my bearing from some great principle of action. Hither to I had been almost wholly the passive creature of circumstances and of constitutional tendency: but I was now called upon to act from choice. I had arrived at a point where the road of life forked out in several different directions and I had to make an election of my path: and no man, I apprehend, whose mind is not below or considerably above the safe level of common sense will deny I had the liberty of exercising an influence on my subsequent life. It was in my power under certain disagreeable restrictions, to be sure, but still it was in my power to go to college. It was equally in my power to go to an inferior institution, which was recommended to me, in the country, where the living was cheap and where I should have lived in a less degree of personal dependence.[9]

8. The line from Pope is from his translation of the *Odyssey* 10:26.

9. It is unclear what was the identity of this other institution. One possibility is General Theological Seminary, which was being organized in 1817. It also may refer to the Episcopal Academy of Connecticut in Chesire, which was founded in 1796 by

For reasons nearly the same, I avoided both these paths and entered on another the most unlikely, in appearance, to conduct me to the goal I had in view. I requested my uncle,[10] as my aunt was about breaking up her school, to use his influence to obtain for me a situation in the customs. He succeeded and late in the fall of 1818 I accepted a desk in the Customs House on a salary of $400 a year. In doing this however I had not the most remote intention of regarding it as a permanency. On the contrary I now felt more confidence in my own resources. I thought I should be able to go on in my studies alone and successfully. I considered the Excise office as a means of independent support allowing time for studious application and resolved to abandon it as soon as my age and other circumstances would admit of my deriving a maintenance from the results of my studies. I acted in this respect with a trust in the Providence of God though certainly without any enlightened view of its operations. The truth, however, of which I had then but a glimpse and which found its chief support in the virtuous feelings of the heart I am now able to approve of in the light of reason and philosophy. Would to God I could refer with the same satisfaction to all my actions! Would to God that every young person could know that while he is walking with a firm trust in providence in the paths of virtue and piety, though he may be utterly unable logically to infold his principles of action and defend them against the shafts of sophistry he is yet guided by those profound truths and holy instincts to which reason after having, in the madness of youth, wasted her energies against them in vain, is, in the soberness of age, glad to recur as to the fixed and ultimate laws of the moral world!

My new employment was so little congenial to my taste that I was almost as much out of my element here as at Moneygripe's. I liked well enough to scribble—but I did most cordially detest every at-

---

Connecticut Episcopalians as a rival to the Congregationalist Yale College. During the second decade of the nineteenth century it was attempting to advance to collegiate status.

10. Edward Seabury (1767–c. 1827).

tempt to use the pen with mechanical precision. And I may here be permitted to mention a trifling incident which illustrates the necessity of vigilance in youthful education in regard to the smallest particulars. Before I was twelve years of age I used to take great pride and pleasure in my handwriting—but one of the first speeches I heard from the teacher of the last school which I attended was that provided a man wrote sense it was of no importance what sort of hand he wrote! From this time I can safely say that I took no pains with my handwriting until a short time before I prepared to enter on the discharge of my present duties. From this species of mechanism there was sometimes an escape in the calculations and accounts of the office, which were often long and complicated and as there was no one who envied me the piece of drudgery I generally succeeded in obtaining it. There was one other thing which rendered my situation particularly uncomfortable. I was extremely sensitive to ridicule to one variety of which: in the shape of teasing I was continually exposed: and my manners being too stiff to evade it and my feelings too strong to submit to it I was sometimes involved in petty difficulties with the other clerks of the office. Persons of such peculiarities are seldom happy unless they mingle with associates who acknowledge those dignified restraints which refined feelings and good sense have imposed on the higher classes of Society.

This year was far from being a profitable one to my studies. Had I possessed a persevering activity of mind I might perhaps have made some valuable attainment in learning. But my mind was constitutionally indolent: it was now perhaps predisposed to relapse in consequence of its former exertions and this indolent disposition was aggravated by a want which has shed, I am sure, a permanent withering influence on my character and happiness—the want, I mean, of a congenial sphere to play in at a time of life when the human energies are particularly buoyant, when the mind is expanding into a new sphere and instinctively craves for new enjoyments. Still I was not entirely stationary. I read some Latin and occasionally a chapter in the Greek Testament but unfortunately I had become too much satisfied with what I had acquired to go through the drudgery to which I had before submitted . Faber on the prophecies was accidentally thrown in my way and I perused it with some other miscellaneous reading which I have now forgotten.[11] But my greatest improvement of mind at this period consisted in efforts which I still made to improve myself in English Composition. In this respect I adopted a plan which I had somewhere seen recommended and which I venture in my turn to recommend to others. It was to turn the psalms or some other plain English writings into verse. I had never the vanity to imagine that I was any thing of a poet but I did believe and still think that this habit gave me a command of words which I should not otherwise have possessed. To be sure a command of words is not enough to form a style—but it is one requisition towards it. My prose style at this period and for sometime afterwards was the most tumid and bombastic imaginable. But this is a fault natural to youth: and I doubt whether my ultimate style would have been ulitmately bettered had this rank, yet natural luxuriance, been suddenly checked by the unsparing pruning knife of a Belles-Lettres Professor. Let the fault be cautiously pointed out to the student and good models and true principles placed before him. In time the vicious habit will be found to have spent itself and to have left the mind better acquainted than it otherwise would have been with the resources of its language. It is thus with many diseases of mind and body—nature, left to herself, works her own cure: she may be assisted by the skilful physician, but she suffers under every attempt at control from the ignorant amd presuming empiric. Speaking of Belles-Lettres reminds me that in the summer of 1819 I read Rollin

11. George Stanley Faber wrote numerous works on the prophecies. Among them were *A General and Connected View of the Prophecies Relative to the Conversion, Restoration, Union, and Future Glory of the Houses of Judah and Israel* . . . , 2 vols. (1808); *A Dissertation on the Prophecies, that have been Fulfilled, are now Fulfilling, or will Hereafter be Fulfilled Relative to the Great Period of the 1260 Years* . . . , 3 vols. (1814–18); and *A Dissertation on the Prophecy Contained in Daniel ix, 24–27* . . . (London, 1811).

on Education.[12] I have never seen it since but from my recollection I think it must be superior to Blair or any other in common use.[13] At the same house too where I was a transient boarder I read Ferguson's Astronomy.[14]

In the spring of 1819 a Confirmation was held in (St. Paul's) the church which I had been in the regular habit of attending and as I them complied with the ordinance I have reserved to this time all reference to my religious feelings, principles and habits. From the time of my previous preparation for this ordinance my attachment for the church in whose bosom I was nurtured continued unabated. For the two years preceding the time of which I am now speaking my religious reading was chiefly such books as Jones' Essay on the church, Jones' Figurative Language and Seabury's Sermons—to which I may add for its devotional influence Taylor's Holy Living and Holy Dying.[15] The former of these carried my notions of church Constitution to the extreme: while the latter which would have proved an admirable corrective to the mental dissipation inseparable from Social life tended rather to increase that acerbity of devotion to which my recluse habits and constitutional temperament pre-

12. This work was also referred to in the previous chapter: Charles Rollin, *The Method of Teaching and Studying the Belles Lettres*.

13. Hugh Blair (1718–1800) was professor of Belles Lettres at Edinburgh and wrote the standard eighteenth-century text on the subject, *Lectures on Rhetoric and Belles Lettres*, originally published in 1783.

14. James Ferguson(1710–76), *Astronomy Explained upon Sir Issac Newton's Principles*. The work was first published in 1756 and was reissued in revised forms until the 1820s.

15. William Jones of Nayland's, *An Essay on the Church* was an apologetical standard for early nineteenth-century Episcopalians. The work of the same author *Lectures on the Figurative Language of the Holy Scripture* was more controversial. It argued the thesis set forth early in the eighteenth century by John Hutchinson that Hebrew was the primitive language of all mankind and when properly interpreted provided all knowledge. The other two works refered to in the text are Samuel Seabury, *Discourses on Several Important Subjects* . . . (New York, 1798), and Jeremy Taylor, *Holy Living and Holy Dying: Together With Prayers Containing the Complete Duty of a Christian*, composed 1650–51.

disposed me. When in addition to this frame of mind the reader recollects my veneration for antiquity and of the Latin language in particular he will not be surprised to learn that my partialities inclined considerably towards the Roman Catholic Church. I carried these partialities however to an extreme that excited both surprise and regret. I attended High Mass on their great days and I need hardly add that the imposing pomp of their worship had the same effect on me that it has had on thousands of others to enkindle the flame of ignorant devotion. I visited their churches not seldom on the Lord's day and was gratified by their preaching. Often have I arisen early in the morning to be present at their Mass—and as there were sometimes but very few I have sometimes wondered that I did not attract the attention of the priest. From being simply an attendent I began to enter into the worship. I procured a mass book and used to follow the priest as nearly as I could; and I even went so far (proh pudor!)[16] as to touch my finger in the holy water, bow at the crucifix and impress the cross on my forehead![17] Of course this was not a blind devotion in relation to the emblematic character of these particular forms. I regarded the water as an emblem of the cleansing efficacy of the Holy Spirit and in applying it in the form of a cross to my forehead expressed the humble prayer that the Spirit of God would appropriate to myself the merits of the Redeemer. This or rather some such meaning (for all these emblems are fertile with various significance) generally passed my mind. I learned also to defend their doctrines. The charge of Image worship I denounced as preposterous. On Papal Infallibility I placed a rational construction: and even the absurdity of Transubstantiation I explained away with a great deal of metaphysical jargon about *substance* and *accidents*.[18] To

16. "O shame!"

17. All of these Roman Catholic ceremonies were considered terribly superstitious and idolatrous at the time by Episcopalians, as well as by other American Protestants.

18. The doctrine of transubstantiation maintained that at the mass the true nature or substance of the bread and wine were transformed into the body and blood of Jesus while the outward physical properties of the bread (or accidents) remain unchanged. This explanation, which hinged upon an inversion of Aristotelian metaphysics, was

the doctrine of purgatory I became a sincere convert and seldom failed, in my private prayers, to recal[l] the images of my departed friends. This last notion I was unhappily able to defend on what those with whom I chiefly argued acknowledged as good authority—my grandfather's sermons, and I have often thought that if the moral influence of a doctrine were the sole test of its truth there was something so soothing and grateful in mingling the images of the departed with one's secret devotions as to constitute for this doctrine, in one view of it at least, a respectable claim on attention.[19] In a word I became a staunch advocate [of] Catholicism: so much so as considerably to alarm my father who had himself a considerable *penchant* the same way. And I verily believe that had I then numbered a single Roman Catholic, of any grade, among my acquaintances I should have been soon enrolled among her holy children. To be sure I may now console myself with the example of the historian of the Decline and Fall;[20] though I desire to be much more thankful that the revulsion, in my own case, has not been, in its lasting consequences, quite so extreme as in his.

I desire however to thank the preserving providence of God that I was not at this dangerous period quite so much carried away as to lose a preference for my own church or a sense of obligation to conform to its worship. Instead of actually entering the country of Catholicism I preferred carrying church pretensions as close as possi-

---

usually dismissed by Anglican writers at the time as being foolish at best and superstitious at worst.

19. Bishop Seabury, in a discourse entitled "The Descent of Christ into Hell," defended the existence of an intermediate state for the departed, where they would await final resurrection. While in that state, he concluded, they could benefit from the prayers of those still alive. See, *Discourses on Several Subjects*, 2 vols. (Hudson, 1815), 1:194–201.

20. Edward Gibbon, the author of the *Decline and Fall of the Roman Empire*, at fifteen years of age while at Magdalen College, Oxford, converted to Roman Catholicism. He later returned to Protestantism and finally became highly skeptical of any revealed religion. In the *Decline and Fall* he bitterly attacked superstition and gave a naturalistic reading of the rise of Christianity. For nineteenth-century Protestants he became a symbol of the connection between Romanism and skepticism.

ble to its border: though to be sure this was not much nearer than the general drift of my religious education had encouraged.[21] The point of my religious character at this time was a fervent but recluse devotion; and in solitude, temperament and the sort of books I read I have traced it to its sources. It will be observed that from the time I originally left home I had not cultivated an acquaintance with any person out of my own family and there was no prospect, in my present situation, of finding a religious friend even if I had thought of such a thing as desiring one—which I did not. I had no other conversations of religion than occasionally an earnest but temperate argument with two or three persons in the office who were deistically inclined though not quite so coarse as [?][22] in their exhibitions of it.

The nature of my preparation for confirmation will thus be easily imagined. It was deeply devotional. My views of religious truth were substantially the same as at the former time of preparation, only more fully developed: my feelings of devotion were of the same general kind, but much stronger. It never occured to me [to] seek the conversation of a clergyman: nor did I once imagine that my new views of human duty or divine requirement could be presented to my mind. Soon after confirmation I partook of the Communion. At my father's request I called upon bishop H[obart] in person to announce my desire to this effect. He encouraged the desire and gave me his best wishes but no particular conversation ensued.

The fabric of my religion was about to be shaken and I have therefore been the more particular in bringing its structure to view. Its strength consisted chiefly in devotion: and devotion was likely to be supplanted if other passions were excited.[23] At the foundations of faith I had never looked unless a few common place arguments on

21. Seabury's grandfather was well known for his attempt to emphasize the Catholic heritage of the Episcopal Church, and the diocese of New York, was at the time a stronghold of this sentiment.

22. Seabury's handwriting is here undecipherable, yet he evidently is contrasting his friends with a grosser proponent of Deism.

23. In the margin of the manuscript Seabury inscribed the word "alter" next to this sentence.

Letter Ten

the external evidences of Christianity deserve that name: of course my house was not fit to withstand the winds and rain of Infidelity. Religion consists of *feeling* and *principle* and it is the well balanced union of the two that constitutes the ανηρτελνος—or perfect man in Christ Jesus.[24] When separated or existing in undue proportions the religious character is more or less weak and defective. By devotion I understand the concentration of religious feeling. If not an original passion, at least it takes the place of one. In reflection on my own mind and observation on the character of others I am persuaded that devotion, though a characteristic feature, is in itself no sure evidence of genuine piety. True piety there cannot be without devotion, but devotion [(]sincere and well meant devotion[)] may exist without piety. I believe that the Buccaneers, the Bedouin Arabs and such others were really and truly devout. I have known men of gross sensuality and great avarice that I believed to be honestly devout: self deceived doubtless but with no other idea of deceiving others by their religious professions. How is this? Devotion must be regarded as a mere passion and as such it has a natural affinity for the leading passion of the mind, be it love, avarice, or whatever else, assimilates with it and strengthens it. Religion of principle leads to rectitude. It is often unamiable but always safe. Religion of feeling produces devotion; it is often amiable but seldom safe.—[The devotion alone may continue after all else that is good has been exploded.][25] Religion reared on the basis of conscience unites the two and is the religion which in young minds should be carefully cherished.

24. Greek for "perfect man." This is perhaps a reference to Ephesians 4:13, "Till we all come in the unity of the faith, and of the knowledge of the Son of God, unto a perfect man, unto the measure of the stature of the fulness of Christ."
25. This sentence has been crossed out in the manuscript.

Eleven

Among the clerks in the Custom House was one who resided at Brooklyn. He had been recently married and was to commence keeping house on the first of May (1819). He was a young man of good family and some amiable traits of character and as some changes were about taking place among my friends I proposed to this gentleman that he should receive me as a boarder. He consented and I accordingly moved my quarters to Brooklyn. Among his acquaintances at this place was one whose oddity was a source of amusement to him and whom he invited one day to tea by way of introducing him to me. He kept a small school with considerable reputation as a teacher but he had within a few years as I understood fallen into careless and dissipated habits to the injury of his business as well as himself.[1] I found A——— a singular being. He had so many ridiculous eccentricities as to render him an object almost of derision and yet he possessed attainments and other good qualities that entitled him to respect. I cannot enlarge on his eccentricities though they might be illustrated by some humorous anecdote. We used frequently to see one another and I found his conversation entertaining and instructive though not always and in the sense in which these terms are usually taken. He was by birth a Welchman [sic]—had come to this country at about seventeen—and by his industry and frugality had laid up a few thousand dollars. He had

1. According to Henry R. Stiles, *A History of Brooklyn*, 3 vols. (Brooklyn, N.Y., 1869), Seabury had been an assistant at a school run by a "Mr. Evan Beynon on Concord Street." Stiles described Beynon as an "excellent scholar" and "a good teacher," as well as a "great admirer of Thomas Paine" (2:90, 115). According to W. J. Rorabaugh, intemperance among school teachers was far from uncommon. See *The Alcoholic Republic: An American Tradition* (New York: Oxford University Press, 1979), 145.

once attempted the study of divinity in the Presbyterian Church but soon gave it up and afterwards joined the Episcopal Church—but at the time I knew him was in the habit of attending no place of public worship. He had become tired of his business, neglected it and in turn, was fast forsaking him. His school consisted of under five and twenty scholars—partly girls and part boys. He was particularly famous for his success with small children and he had now two [or] three of about seven years of age whom he was about introducing to the Latin Grammar calculating to carry them as far as Caesar's Commentaries when he generally gave them into other hands. He made me an offer of the school if I would take it off his hands, and though I felt my age to be a serious objection being but little more that eighteen yet fearing that I should not soon obtain so good an opening again I consented and on the first [of] August 1819 left the Custom House and entered on what seemed to have been the predestined business of my life at Brooklyn.

I ought previously to have mentioned that with a view to some employment of this kind I had during the summer months engaged Mr. Brouse whom the reader may remember was first introduced to me at N.'s as an excellent classical scholar to hear [for] me a few recitations in Latin and Greek. My object was chiefly to acquire a correct habit of pronunciation in which I partially succeeded and which was all the benefit I derived from Brouse.

I must give the reader an idea of Brouse. He was not much above five feet in height. His head, in its outward dimensions, was wonderfully capacious: projecting over in front, behind and on both sides so that his boys used to compare it to an umbrella. His forehead in particular was so ample that the elevation of one eyebrow nearly an inch above the other was a deformity that you scarcely observed. His voice was harsh and strong and when exerted with any effort was absolutely terrific. By way of compensation for the shortness of his stature nature as usual had given him an ample fund of vanity. Unfortunately too he was ambitious to excel on subjects for [which] he was most unfitted: and I shall never forget the strange grimaces, the theatrical starts, and the tremendous vocal explosions with which, as a display of rhetorical powers, he once recited to me the lovely poem of the Lady of the Lake! His memory was prodigious and as he was fond of the theatre he would of[ten] give us a treat of this kind though I remember nothing that equalled in ludicrous effect, the manner which he would clasp his hands, turn up his disjointed eyes and lower his voice with a crackling tenor as he uttered the beautiful lines

> If there exist on earth a tear
> From passion's dross etc.,[2]

B. had too a most unblushing front. Nothing could repel him. He took much pains to court my acquaintance frequently visiting me at Brooklyn. He called himself a Universalist—but I discovered after a while that his habits were exceedingly licentious.

A and B were both pedagogues in fact and by profession: congeneric but of individual varieties. Both believed in the birch: but A kept [it] in reserve as a last appeal while B used it incessantly, enforcing with it everything that he said and in proportion as one degree of it lost its influence by familiarity rising to another till he had arrived at the most enormous excesses. A. cultivated *passion* on principle because he thought that occasional bursts of it had a good effect: B. was perpetually boisterous. A.'s school was generally still and when occasionally a buzz was heard, the tap of his pencil or penknife was sure to make all around quake with fear and be silent as death. B.'s school was forever a hubbub—but then his own voice often broke out like a clap of thunder above the roaring of the winds. It was diverting to see B. strutting round [like] the character of Ajax among his Grecians,[3] stamping with his foot, breaking a mahogany ruler

2. This is from Sir Walter Scott's *Lady of the Lake*, canto II, lines 467–68. Seabury is quoting it from memory. It should read, "And if there be a human tear / From passion's dross refined and clear."

3. Ajax, son of Telamon in the *Iliad*, was, next to Achilles, the most distinguished and bravest of the Greeks, standing head and shoulder above them in stature.

with a blow on a pine desk or a dunce's head as chance might be, and roaring "silence!" with a burst of sound that was enough to annihilate the timid goddess forever:[4] but it was almost equally so to see A. turn around with a slow pedantic air, dart around him his flashing eye, and having restored order with a look of terror or at most a word resume with solemn gravity the immediate object of his attention.

These were the two geniuses under whose auspices I may be said to have commenced my social career. I cannot be said to have *selected* them as companions: for I had no acquaintances from whom to make a selection. My initimacy with them was, in the one case wholly and in the other in part, the necessary result of circumstances. It was however gradually formed and at least a year elapsed before I understood their characters.

From the fall of 1819 to the fall of 1820 there [was] no material change in my habits of mind or conduct. In the winter of 1819–20 I used to rise between three and four o'clock in the morning and read Paley's Moral Philosophy. I was incompetent to estimate his fundamental position: or rather I had no suspicion that it was disputed and I received it as a something to be *learned* not investigated.[5] It was my habit after having read every chapter twice over to write it down from memory. I can recall some miscellaneous reading of this period

4. This reference is unclear. It is possibly an oblique reference to the goddess Eirene (of peace) or Pax in Latin who as personified by a draped maiden holding a sheaf of wheat and a statuette of abundance. Similarly, it could refer to Tacita, the minor Roman goddess of silence, who was often associated with Harpocrates, the god who enjoined silence by putting his finger to his lips.

5. By the decade of the 1820s Paley's *Moral Philosophy* was being criticized on many grounds. Paley's philosophy was largely utilitarian in its appeal and, according to its critics, depended too much on selfish motives. The only difference between duty and prudence, for example, for Paley was that "in the one case, we consider what we shall gain or lose in the present world; in the other case, we consider also what we shall gain or lose in the world to come." (*The Principles of Moral and Political Philosophy* . . . [New York, 1831], 43). Furthermore, he offered an account of moral obligation that was inadequate from the perspective of the proponents of the competing system of the Scottish Common Sense school.

but nothing else that was really an object of study. In the summer I took lessons with B. in Italian but never pursued it with any interest. Indeed though never absolutely sick my health was far from good: I was depressed habitually with a lassitude: the nature and treatment of which I did not understand but the effect of which was to render me good for nothing. Two causes combined with this to retard my classical studies in particular. B. had the reputation of being a superior classical scholar and I saw that he knew nothing which I either had not attained or thought I might attain at any time. I.xxx[6] also enjoyed the same reputation and from a slight acquaintance I found that he was a mere smatterer. I understood also that clergymen, even those of respectable standing, pushed their acquirements in Greek no further than the Testament. I had energy enough to rise to the level of those about me and too much indolence to rise above it. These persons became my standard: I knew nothing of the value of study as a mere discipline and if I had it is doubtful whether I should have been disposed to submit to it: it was not unnatural therefore that I should have been so far satisfied with my acquisitions as to put off the augmentation of my stock to a more convenient season. Here I was wrong and in this as well as a thousand other cases have had reason to rue my folly.

It might have been in the fall of 1819 but I think it was in the fall of 1820 that A. becoming tired of his lounging habits proposed to join me in the charge of the school: promising in answer to the only objection I made that his habits in many respects should be changed. We agreed to this regulation: and I never saw a man who in an instant, as it were, was so entirely altered. He was a man of singular constitution. Brandy and tobacco which he had used rather freely rendered him easy and indolent: the moment these stimulants were laid aside he was all activity and vigor. Before this period we frequently referred to religious topics: he expressed his dissent from my views but never brought any argument to shake my confidence

6. This is the first and only reference to this figure in Seabury's text.

in them. But after this period the case was wholly different. He brought to every subject a keenness of mind and copiousness of argument that fairly baffled me. His favorite topic was one of which before I had never heard and had only read of as a strange and exploded notion: that was *materialism*. Matter and motion were enough he thought to explain all the phenomena of thought; in consequence he denied the immortality of the soul. Occasionally he would argue in the same way against the doctrine of special providence and the reasonableness of prayer.[7] In short he was a Deist and when in the proper frame of mind by no means unskilful in the use of his weapons.

Before I explain the effect that A.'s arguments had on my mind I will carry the remainder of my story to its close. A.'s connection with me in business ceased in the Spring following [that is, 1821] and I afterwards continued alone. I gradually entered more and more into Society until my spare time was almost equally divided between social amusements and studies. My devotion to study was irregular and fitful though seldom entirely suspended. My business compelled me to familiarize my mind with Algebra and Geometry, etc., and to revise and extend my classical studies. On subjects connected with English grammar and English pronunciation A. was an acute critic: I was thus induced to study these subjects with particular attention, the benefit of which I have always experienced not only in the knowledge acquired but in the habits of criticism which I transferred to subjects that A. never aspired to. I said that when I took the school it presented the monstrous incongruity of a male and female assemblage conjoined. One of my first plans was to render it merely a school for boys which I effected as soon as was practicable. There was also in the place a select classical school for boys. My next plan was to bring about a conjunction between my own and this: and by

7. Special providence was the belief that God acted in nature not only in ordinary ways, that is through the stated laws of operation, but also through special means, such as the answering of prayer, which if not strictly miraculous, were nonetheless extraordinary and hence a departure from the regular course of events.

carrying two or three boys, whom I had, over a quantity sufficient of Latin and Greek, in such a manner, as to obtain the good opinion of a few favorable judges in the place, I succeeded in accomplishing the project. There was very little more incident in my life: anything further that I could say would be rather the history of my opinions. This task, God willing, I will perform on some other occasion. There was enough of incident however to give continuity to such a story whenever I attempt it. Intercourse with the world had a happy effect on me: it increased my knowledge of men: released me in a great degree from my stiffness of manners; brought out my social faculties and invigorated my mind. *Amici fures temporis* may be applied to social visits in general and I often used to denounce them by severer epithets.[8] But my case, in this respect, as in many others, was anomalous and I believe that the time I have spent in society has been as profitable as any part of my life. True I might have secured all the advantages of social intercourse with vastly less sacrifice of time: but when is the life that appears in the retrospect well proportioned? It was in the fall of 1820 [(]or rather winter[)] that I read Stackhouse['s] Hist[ory] of the Bible and Patrick's Com[mentary]. In the winter following I read St. Paul's Epistles with Lock's [*sic*] Commentary.[9]

It is wonderful how the defects of the mind sometimes become the source of improvement. This is one disadvantage of a regular education: the mind never feels its own wants: it has no deep and practical sense of ignorance: it never realizes the need of knowledge. It is thus with religion: the child that is educated in the bosom of a pious family cannot form those profound convictions of sinfulness and

8. "Friends are thieves of time." The proverb is from Francis Bacon.
9. Thomas Stackhouse (1677–1752), *A New History of the Holy Bible, from the Beginning of the World to the Establishment of Christianity. With Answers to Most of the Controversial Questions, Dissertations upon the Most Remarkable Passages, and a Connection with Profane History All Along* (1737); John Locke (1632–1704), *A Paraphrase and Notes on the Epistles of St. Paul* (published posthumously, 1705–07). Simon Patrick (1626–1707) wrote paraphrases of the books of the Bible from Genesis through the Song of Solomon. They were included (and generally read) in Robert Lowth, et al., *A Critical Commentary and Paraphrase on the Old and New Testaments and the Apocrypha*. . . .

that clear perception of the happy and necessary influence of revealed truth as one that has become, in the school of the world, experimentally acquainted with all the weaknesses of his nature and after long groping, espies the light of the gospel from his dark abyss. Necessity spurs the mind. A man may perform a dark and infrequent journey by the light of a small taper and with a few directions on paper. But if he is compelled to set off without these or by any mishap is deprived of them it is ten to one but he brings fire out of the woods or stones around him, travels over ten times the ground he need and returns with a tolerably accurate chart of the whole and his wits wonderfully sharpened by the necessity that compelled him to construct it. I do not wish to underate [*sic*] the benefits of a regular education: it would be a presumptuous risque in any parent or child to decline them. But I must say that I believe I owe the most of my knowledge and my best habits of mind to my profound ignorance at a time when, in the ordinary course of things, a college education would have afforded me just light enough to pass along the road of life without perplexity. It required very little learning to answer A.'s arguments. I might have said to him, "you escape one difficulty only to be entangled in a worse one: you know as little of the essence of matter as of Mind: your materialism leads to, or rather is the necessary offspring of a mechanical philosophy that strips God of all his moral attributes: besides as to practice the doctrine is of little importance: God may confer immortality on matter as well as on spirit"—such sort of answers would have carried him out of his depth or driven him to consequences by which he was not prepared to abide: and such answers might have been *learned* from any School treatise on Psychology.[10] But obvious as these answers would be to any one that had *learned* them—they were out of my reach: I had never heard of them: I knew not where to find them: and as the subject was of vital

10. As Seabury acknowledges, such a refutation of Deism was by no means original. Deism was frequently attacked by showing that the principle of skepticism that the Deists used against revelation also potentially undermined their confidence in natural religion.

importance I was obliged to descend and explore the bowels of the earth and dig for the gold of truth.

The insulated question of materialism was first examined. I will not dwell on the arguments nor on the fallacies in them which I subsequently discovered. I will only say that I was at first captivated and afterwards converted by them to a belief of the doctrine. But the mere question of the nature of the soul did not long detain me. My reading and reasoning compelled me to push it to its consequences and I soon found myself an advocate of the mechanical philosophy and having first denied human accountability was led to reject a belief in God as a Creator and Judge. These a priori deductions superceded the outward evidences of Christianity. There is a kindred in error as well as truth: one doubt suggests another. I felt convinced I had rational doubts—was it reasonable I asked, to demand my *belief* unless the proof amounted to certainty? I thought clearly not—and thus felt secure in the reasonableness of skepticism at least if not of positive infidelity. Thus the bulwarks of faith were demolished. Prayer, if continued at all, was merely a habit—the notion of Providence was always distrusted and sometimes scouted.

This frame of mind lasted nearly two years: not always in a state of absolute infidelity but in a state of *distrust*. All thoughts of the ministry were virtually abandoned; so much so that I made no effort to save my grandfather's library which was sold about this time, thinking I should never want it. One question presented itself of great interest—should I continue my apparent connexion with the church? I hardly knew how to decide. I submitted the question to a judicious lay friend, opening to him the state of my mind; and acting on his advice continued to approach the communion in the best frame of mind I could. There was a continual struggling within. But the drift of my reasoning led me to regard this as the effect of early prejudice—and not as the voice of God speaking through the holy instincts of nature.

But though my courage was proof against all these consequences in the abstract I confess I was apalled when I began to realize them in fact. Moral obligation was destroyed. The social ties were riven asunder. Parental affection, filial duty, conjugal fidelity, honesty, gratitude, all that dignify the species and endear them to one another, were at the mercy of self interest or at best of conventional agreement. And what had I gained? I denied a creator and placed the creation upon a turtle's back.[11] The reflection naturally occurred— here I am in a wilderness, a wood, a swamp. Have I not lost my road? Have I not taken a wrong path? I was not long in setting off in another direction. I studied the external evidences of Christianity: Grotius, Butler, Paley, Chalmers, every book I could find, I read.[12] I started every objection I could myself and gleaned all the objections of others—and for every objection I found an answer. Again I recurred to the foundations of religion. I thought much on the doctrine of final causes.[13] I read Paley's Natural Theology.[14] Was it reasonable, I asked, that all these intelligible marks of wisdom and contrivance should be set aside by a little abstract reasoning? The negative answer gradually gained strength in my mind. And again even supposing that the apparent proofs of final causes may be explained as mechanical principles is it not reasonable to believe that an Intelligent Cause existed prior to the mechanical? If so is it not reasonable to believe that this Intelligible Cause should be revealed to man [never] more clearly than by his nature works? If such a revelation is offered

11. In various mythologies, for example that found among some of the North American Indian tribes, the world was pictured as being supported on the back of a turtle.

12. Hugo Grotius (1583–1645), *De Veritate Religionis Christianae* (1622); Joseph Butler (1692–1752), *The Analogy of Religion, Natural and Revealed, to the Constitution and Course of Nature* (1736); William Paley (1743–1805), *A View of the Evidences of Christianity* (1794); Thomas Chalmers (1780–1847), *The Evidence and Authority of the Christian Revelation* . . . (1814). All of these works attempted to prove the truthfulness of revealed religion by an appeal to nature.

13. Final causes concern the end or purpose of a thing.

14. William Paley, *Natural Theology: or Evidences of the Existence and Attributes of the Deity, Collected from the Appearances of Nature* (1802). This work is perhaps most famous for its opening pages which compare the design of the universe with a watch found on a beach.

133

should it not be thankfully received? Are not the proofs satisfactory that the bible is such a Revelation? May we not believe then in the authority of the bible that this Intelligent Cause is a Moral Governor and Judge? and still more easily believe the almost inevitable consequence that we are his accountable and immortal subjects?

One great difficulty long remained. If these truths are necessary to be believed why is not the evidence greater? But the more I knew of my heart the better able I was to answer this question satisfactorily. I could not deny that much native corruption, in the shape of vanity, pride and presumption had mingled with my unbelief. I saw that *belief* and *unbelief* required different soils and produced different fruits. Hence I came slowly but firmly to the conclusion that moral truth was so exhibited to our minds as to become a *test of character*: and that the evidence *could not have been greater consistently with moral agency*. Certainty would have produced blind conformity and obedience: it would have made us machines.

These subjects possess no great interest for common minds. They were well termed in the Scholastic philosophy *transcendental*: they *lie beyond* ordinary consciousness.[15] It is therefore of little use to dwell on them. Let me rather be thankful that after roaming over the waters of the great abyss I had strength given me to return into the ark from which I had flown. And let others profit by such examples! Let them yield a manly deference to the authority of the wise and good! If they doubt let them examine with caution and reverence; not with precipitancy and rashness.

15. Transcendental was a term applied by the medieval philosophers to predicates which by their universal application were considered to transcend the Aristotelian categories of predicaments.

Index

Index